A Lawyer's
Wellbeing c
Managing S

ANGUS LYON

Head of legal publishing
Fiona Fleming

Publisher
Helen Donegan

Editor
Laura Slater

Published by ARK Group:

UK, Europe and Asia office
6–14 Underwood Street
London, N1 7JQ
United Kingdom
Tel: +44(0) 207 566 5792
publishing@ark-group.com

North America office
4408 N. Rockwood Drive, Suite 150
Peoria IL 61614
United States
Tel: +1 (309) 495 2853
publishingna@ark-group.com

www.ark-group.com

Layout by Susie Bell, www.f-12.co.uk

Printed by Canon (UK) Ltd, Cockshot Hill, Reigate, RH2 8BF, United Kingdom

ISBN: 978-1-78358-221-1

A catalogue record for this book is available from the British Library

© 2015 ARK Group

All rights reserved. No part of this publication may be reproduced or transmitted in
any form or by any means, except in accordance with the provisions of the Copyright,
Designs and Patents Act 1988 or under terms of a licence issued by the Copyright
Licencing Agency in respect of photocopying and/or reprographic reproduction.
Application for permission for other use of copyright material, including permission
to reproduce extracts in other published works, should be made in writing to the
publishers. Full acknowledgement of author, publisher, and source must be given.

DISCLAIMER
This publication is intended as a general guide only. The information and opinions it
contains are not intended to provide legal advice. The publishers bear no responsibility
for any errors or omissions contained herein.

ARK Group is a division of Wilmington plc. The company is registered in England &
Wales with company number 2931372 GB. Registered office: 6-14 Underwood Street,
London N1 7JQ. VAT Number: GB 899 3725 51.

Contents

Part 2: Me

Part 3: You

Part 4: Do

Executive summary

All lawyers will experience stress and challenges to their mental wellbeing at some point in their career. Not all stress is bad, of course; in many circumstances, it can provide a positive drive and motivation. But stress is subjective, and one person's motivational stress is another person's intolerable pressure. Mental health, moreover, is still often associated with significant issues of stigma within the legal profession. Lawyers are busy people and nobody wishes to be seen as a weak link in the chain of a professional practice.

Lawyers are frequently exposed to a stressful environment and challenging mental conditions due to the nature of their work. There are certain organisations to help with this. In the UK, for example, LawCare works with lawyers to provide assistance in coping with the pressures of a legal career. Their work highlights the issues that exist for UK lawyers. At present, LawCare's advisory and support service receives around 2,000 calls per year from troubled lawyers. By far the most common issue reported is stress, representing 75 per cent of the calls received. This is followed by depression at 12 per cent, alcohol related problems at 5 per cent, and other varied issues making up the remainder of calls.

UK lawyers do not suffer alone. In the US, a recent study by the American Bar Association showed that depression (50 per cent) and anxiety (21 per cent) accounted for the largest part of lawyers' mental health problems, suggesting that what we call 'stress' may be a coverall term for a variety of problems.

About two thirds of LawCare's callers are able to identify a specific cause of their problem, the most significant being 'workload' at 27 per cent, 'disciplinary issues' at 20 per cent, 'bullying' at 15 per cent, and 'financial problems' at 14 per cent. (Other issues included ethical problems, redundancy, relationship problems, and bereavement.)

The pressures on lawyers are multifactorial. A large number of prominent academics and lawyers have considered these issues in the last decade, and there is a vast body of literature out there on the topic – but there is a large gulf between knowledge and practice. This book is therefore structured as a comprehensive framework within which we can think about mental wellbeing and stress. As well as contributing to the wider general discussion on wellbeing for lawyers, it provides practical guidance about steps that can be taken by lawyers to help themselves and to improve their workplace environment as a whole. It addresses what can be done to facilitate healthy workplaces and practices to enhance creativity and productivity.

The book is divided into four parts. Part 1 ('So what?') sets the scene. Parts 2–4 then set out a model to help readers think about wellbeing from the perspectives of the individual ('Me'), the individual in two-person relationships and in groups ('You'), and to consider the impact of events that go on around us ('Do'). The idea of 'ME.YOU.DO' is proposed to help readers think about the issues in a simple, yet comprehensive, way.

Chapter 1 introduces the concept of 'wicked problems' – social problems that defy solution – and it considers the increasing problem of mental illness in the legal profession in this light. A number of reports have been produced on behalf of various branches of the profession in recent years addressing lawyers' wellbeing and this chapter looks at some of these and highlights common themes and challenges. It explores stress from various perspectives: historical, engineering, stigma, and psychological, with the aim of clarifying a working definition of a misunderstood concept. Contrary to much popular myth, 'stress' *can* be good for us.

Chapter 2 covers the area of 'prehab'; that is, practical steps that can be taken in 'prehabilitation' to avoid the need, at a later stage, for rehabilitation. It is informed by 'reverse therapy', the understanding and application of principles of psychotherapy to enhance wellbeing and build resilience to mental illness.

Many lawyers share characteristics which enhance legal competence, but which can also predispose them to related psychological pressures. A rehabilitation programme for burnt-out professionals in the United States provides treatment for individuals and points towards a way of thinking about lawyers' mental health proactively, as well as reactively.

While the first part of the book outlines the extent and nature of the challenge that we face in dealing with stress and mental wellbeing as individuals and as a profession, Parts 2–4 provide a framework for thinking about and coping with stress and situations impacting our mental health. Each of these parts begins with a case study of a lawyer which illustrates some of the pressures on mental health that are faced in legal practice. Throughout the chapters that follow, we then explore how these can be addressed. Individuals' details in these studies have been anonymised for confidentiality and partly collaged.

Chapter 3 covers areas of basic neurology and physiology. We look at how our brains and bodies assess anxiety, as well as external and internal pressure.

In Chapter 4 we look at aspects of psychological resilience, what it is, and how it can be enhanced. Chapter 5 introduces the concept of 'mentalization' and covers theories of mindfulness and their practical application in aiding greater self-awareness.

In Chapter 6 mentalization is discussed in one-to-one relationships and we think about how a number of closely related concepts of the mind can help us to be more 'other-aware' in legal practice. This is explored further in Chapter 7, in which we think about how we relate in group situations.

Chapter 8 acknowledges that sometimes life hits you where and when you least expect it. It can be hard to separate clients' lives from our own, and at times change can feel almost unmanageable. This chapter is intended to help people who may be confronting unmanageable stress, depression, or grief, and is also intended to be a point of reference for managers or supervisors to help colleagues who are going through a difficult period.

There are always things that can be done to improve the situation, however, and Chapters 9 and 10 explore the active steps we can take to make things different, to become more resilient, and to enhance the wellbeing of those around us.

In conclusion, the Epilogue addresses some institutional aspects of wellbeing in the legal profession and offers some modest proposals for the way forward.

The advice in this book is informed by the author's practical experience as a lawyer and as a therapist. It is also underpinned by statistical and research evidence to support the theories and suggestions shared. This book is for lawyers everywhere – irrespective of location, job level, or type of legal practice. The aim is to provide a practical resource for individual lawyers and for firms and chambers thinking about personal mental health and wellbeing in the workplace generally.

About the author

Angus Lyon has practised as a litigation solicitor for 35 years and since 1987 as a partner in a firm on the Suffolk coast. He has specialised as a claimant personal injury lawyer for the last 20 years and has regularly been recommended in this area of work in the Legal 500. He is a professional deputy.

Partly as a result of his growing work in psychiatric injuries, he developed an interest in psychotherapy and obtained a secondary qualification as a psychodynamic counsellor. He is a registered member of the British Association of Counselling and Psychotherapy and is a director and co-founder of Catalyst Counselling CIC, a social enterprise providing counselling and training in East Anglia. He has been a LawCare volunteer since 2008.

Angus is also a cricketer and has played for Southwold Cricket Club and The Lowestoft Etceteras for a generation. He also plays bass.

Acknowledgements

My thanks to all who have, wittingly or otherwise, informed my writing and helped me to keep my wits. Special thanks to my remarkable colleagues at Catalyst Counselling and Mears Hobbs & Durrant; Elizabeth Rimmer and Anna Buttimore at LawCare; Helen Donegan and Laura Slater at ARK Group; to my father Iain, for consciously pointing me towards the law and for your turn of phrase, and my mother Susan for unconsciously pointing me to psychotherapy and for helping me to see connections; to my family and close friends who help to keep me grounded; and to my clients, who have taught me most.

Dedication

To Susan

Introduction

Wellbeing in the legal profession

Health and wellbeing are near the top of most people's agendas. Even if we do not go to the gym, exercise regularly, or maintain a healthy diet, most of us wish that we did so. This book is written specifically about health and wellbeing for lawyers, and covers the related issues of stress and mental health, which are areas of growing concern within the legal profession.

It is written for lawyers by a lawyer (who also works as a psychotherapist), who understands the particular demands and pressures of a legal career. I have seen first hand the benefits for clients of 'talking therapy'; sometimes, over a period of weeks or years, a person will talk to another and achieve greater clarity, self-awareness, growth, transformation, a lessening or elimination of distress, depression, panic, and obsessiveness, and as a result they are able to live with the stresses and strains of everyday professional life in a healthier and more meaningful way.

Lawyers use their minds continually, exercising their brains to find innovative solutions to client problems, anticipating potential pitfalls and developments in the course of a matter, and in managing and prioritising caseloads. The need to think about and care for our minds and be more aware of the minds of others (whether colleagues, clients, opponents, family, or friends) must be of prime concern. This aspiration was echoed recently in Chrissie Lightfoot's book, *Tomorrow's Naked Lawyer*: 'I… urge any ambitious lawyer who wishes to make and/or maintain a life-long career in the law to embrace a deep(er) understanding of psychology. More importantly, legal education and training providers must build this into the fabric of their educational programmes'.[1]

The challenges of poor mental health in the legal profession have been particularly recognised over the last 10–20 years. Many suggestions have been made as to how the situation might be improved; however, sometimes the very complexity and nature of the problem defies a solution. Lawyers are busy people – time targets have to be met, cases won, clients pleased, regulations complied with, bills paid – and thinking about mental health involves significant issues of stigma. Nobody wishes to be seen as a weak link in the chain of a professional practice.

LawCare

Over the last 20 years LawCare, a charity in the UK, has worked with lawyers to provide assistance for those in the legal professions who feel they have nowhere to turn.[2] At present, the advisory and support service receives around 2,000 calls per year from troubled lawyers.

By far the most common issue that LawCare callers report is that of 'stress', which represents 75 per cent of calls (this is followed by 'depression' and 'alcohol related problems'). The pressures on lawyers are many and varied, and a great deal has been written about external causes of stress. Excessive work demands, pressure from work colleagues, financial worries, and the demands of family and home all play a part. Of those of LawCare's callers who are able to identify a specific cause for their problem (roughly two thirds), those most cited are 'workload' (27 per cent), 'disciplinary issues' (20 per cent), and 'bullying' (15 percent). These external pressures are experienced in the underlying context of one-to-one and group relationships and our own inner thoughts, wishes, feelings, aspirations, and desires. These inter-personal and intra-personal factors can often be overlooked.

These challenges to wellbeing experienced by those in the legal profession reflect pressures experienced in society in general, with one in four individuals in England experiencing a mental health problem during the course of any year. Studies in the United States and Australia, however, have indicated that pressures experienced in the legal profession are perceived to be greater than in the population at large.[3]

Who should read this book?

This book is for lawyers everywhere – whether you are a student, trainee, newly qualified, many years qualified, or near retirement, and whether you practice in Southampton, Swansea, Stirling, Sligo, Seattle, Sydney, Seoul, or somewhere else. The material in this book is informed by my practical experience as a lawyer working in England over the last few decades, and it is illustrated by the personal experiences of lawyers whose stories have been anonymised, deconstructed, and re-arranged for confidentiality.

Lawyers like evidence. Therefore this book is underpinned by statistical and research evidence, particularly from the last 10 years. The statistics worldwide for lawyers' mental health are increasingly gloomy and pessimistic. Perhaps a change in the way we think might create hope and room in the profession for things to improve.

In a recent book on design by Dunne and Raby, the authors express this hope: 'Rather than giving up altogether… there are other possibilities for design: one is to use design as a means of speculating how things could be – speculative design. This form of design thrives on imagination and aims to open up new perspectives on what [are] sometimes called wicked problems, to create spaces for discussion and debate about alternative ways of being…'.[4] This book is intended to create a space for discussion and debate about alternative ways of being lawyers.

Many prominent academics and lawyers have considered these issues in the last decade or so – and there is a vast body of literature out there on this very topic – but there is a large gulf between knowledge and practice. The aim of this book therefore is to provide a practical resource for individual lawyers, firms, and chambers, and for the profession generally, to think about personal mental health and wellbeing in the workplace.

How is this book structured?

The book is structured to look at the three areas of 'Me', 'You', and 'Do', both to provide a comprehensive framework within which we can think about mental wellbeing and stress, and also to provide a simple aide-memoire for those times when we are in the heat of battle and our thinking is not as clear as we would like it to be. We may be just about to go into court and anticipate a bruising cross-examination, going to meet a particularly demanding and difficult client, driving to work and anticipating a meeting from hell, or simply spending a few moments thinking about workload. The idea of 'ME.YOU.DO' is intended to help thinking, and to steady nerves.

Work-related stresses and strains interact with other aspects of our lives, the intra-personal, the inter-personal, and the non-personal. Our experience is multifactorial. The 'intra-personal' is what happens *inside* us: what we think and feel, what we aspire to and what we dream about ('ME'). The 'inter-personal' deals with the ways we relate to other people and the teams and groups that we work and live with: what happens *between* us ('YOU'). The 'non-personal' relates to events and external pressures, the things that have been done to us, what goes on *around* us, and events that we may or may not be able to control in the future: the stuff that happens ('DO').

References

1. Lightfoot, C., *Tomorrow's Naked Lawyer: NewTech, NewHuman, NewLaw*, ARK Group, London, 2014.
2. LawCare's service is provided for all members of the legal profession in the UK, Isle of Man, and Ireland. See: www.lawcare.org.uk.
3. James, C. G., 'Lawyers' Wellbeing and Professional Legal Education', *The Law Teacher: The International Journal of Legal Education, 42*, 2008, pp.85–97.
4. Dunne, A. and Raby, F., *Speculative Everything: Design, Fiction, and Social Dreaming*, MIT Press, Cambridge, MA, 2013.

Part 1:
So what?

Chapter 1:
Stress and mental illness –
A wicked legal problem?

*'I considered going into business or becoming
a lawyer – not for the money, but for the
thrill of problem-solving.'*

Lisa Randall

The statistics

Over the last decade, the issue of mental illness in the legal profession in the UK and worldwide has gained increasing attention. A substantial amount of literature has been published on the topic which emphasises the extent of the problem. There is growing awareness in different areas and branches of the profession of the significance of wellbeing and mental health.

It is undeniable that there can be 'no health without mental health', in the words of the 2011 UK cross-governmental mental health outcomes report.[1] A detailed study carried out recently on behalf of the UK Council for Psychotherapy concluded that good mental health has an even greater role in our overall wellbeing than was previously thought, and that having either depression or anxiety is around five times worse than the worst physical health condition for peoples' subjective wellbeing.[2] However, when one tries to assess the factors that contribute to good mental health, the position becomes complex.

LawCare

In 2012 the charity LawCare conducted a survey into stress in the legal profession.[3] Over 1,000 solicitors and barristers in the UK and Ireland responded. The results showed that three quarters of the lawyers surveyed felt more stressed than they had five years previously. The main reasons given for this were being overloaded with work, management issues (including lack of appreciation), and feeling isolated or unsupported. Other reasons included having unattainable targets, long hours, poor pay, and job insecurity. The majority of those asked (70 per cent) said that they experienced their work environment as stressful. Almost half believed they had insufficient support. About two thirds said that they would be concerned about reporting feelings of stress to an employer. Over two thirds said that they worked late every day or at least several times a week, and just under one third indicated that they occasionally drank more than the recommended units of alcohol per week.

Solicitors

The Law Society of England and Wales' 'Survey of Solicitors Health and Well-being' in 2014 indicated that 96 per cent of solicitors said they experienced negative stress, with 19 per cent at severe or extreme levels.[4] Workload and client expectations were identified as the most common causes of stress in the previous year's report. Despite the number of those experiencing extreme or severe stress, only 5 per cent said that they had taken time off work as a consequence.

The Bar

In April 2015 the Bar Council published a comprehensive and wide-ranging report, entitled 'Wellbeing at the Bar'.[5] The Council was keen to better understand levels of wellbeing across the Bar, and to identify what interventions and resources might be put in place to support practising barristers' general wellbeing. The report revealed that, of those surveyed (about one sixth of the profession), around one in eight barristers felt emotionally exhausted and over a half did not sleep properly. Around two thirds indicated that they thought their present levels of stress had a negative impact on their work performance.

A large number of respondents indicated that most or all of the time they found it difficult to control or stop worrying (33 per cent); tended to dwell on their mistakes (35 per cent); tended to feel nervous, anxious, or on edge (24 per cent); tended to be very critical of themselves (59 per cent); and experienced unpleasant physical symptoms when they felt stressed, for example headache, fatigue, palpitations, upset stomach, and achy muscles (28 per cent).

Financial concerns, devaluation of the profession's reputation in the eyes of the public and government, and long unsociable working hours were perceived as sources of pressure.

The in-house legal sector

In July 2015, LBC Wise Counsel published a report on the wellbeing of in-house lawyers.[6] The author of the report, Paul Gilbert, indicated that he had never been more concerned for the mental wellbeing of the profession. The report observed that in-house lawyers mostly work in small teams, often lack the infrastructure to support their roles, and tend to soak up the pressures placed on them by colleagues with their own stresses to manage. The report highlights the job demands on in-house lawyers to be increasingly efficient, cut costs, and to do more with less. It raises the growing issue of technology blurring boundaries between work and home. Gilbert believes that the pressure on mental wellbeing is the greatest challenge facing in-house legal teams today.

The judiciary

The '2014 UK Judicial Attitude Survey' reported on findings covering salaried judges in England and Wales courts and UK tribunals.[7] The report reveals that the judiciary is experiencing an erosion of social respect and judges feel undervalued by government and media, and that the working conditions have deteriorated over the last five years with caseloads growing significantly. Almost a half of the respondents (46 per cent) indicated that, in their view, their caseload was excessive.

A significant issue putting pressure on the judiciary is that of change. 60 per cent of judges reported that there had either been a large amount of change or that the job had changed completely in recent years. Almost all judges in England and Wales courts and UK tribunals (87 per cent) feel the judiciary need control over changes affecting judges, and 73 per cent believe too much change has been imposed on the judiciary in recent years. While most accept that change is needed within the judiciary, just over half feel that the amount of change in recent years has brought judges to 'breaking point'.

When considering recruitment to the bench, the main reasons judges would encourage suitable people to apply to join the judiciary include the chance to contribute to justice being done, the challenge of the work, intellectual satisfaction, and public service. However, a large number of judges said that they would no longer encourage anyone to apply to become a judge. Financial considerations play a significant part in this view; however, other factors feature highly, including constant policy changes, lack of administrative support, the feeling of being an employee or civil servant, and the social isolation of the job.

A global issue

The issue of wellbeing in the legal profession has been investigated in detail in many countries. By way of brief example, The Brain & Mind Research Institute at the University of Sydney in Australia published a study in 2009 entitled 'Courting the Blues: Attitudes towards depression in Australian law students and lawyers'.[8] It was the first reported study of its kind in Australia and was conducted with the participation of solicitors, barristers, and law students from 13 universities.

The study revealed high levels of psychological distress and the risk of depression in the students and practising lawyers who participated when compared with Australian community norms and other tertiary student groups. Participants revealed a number of attitudes and behaviours which implied a general reluctance to seek help for mental health issues. These included negative attitudes and stigmatising views towards mental illness; the view that people with mental illness are likely to be discriminated against by their employers and others; low levels of confidence in mental health professionals; and the generally low level of knowledge of issues relating to mental illness amongst a substantial proportion of the sample. Generally, these data implied a reluctance to seek help from mental health professionals.

This report was followed, two years later, by a detailed report by the Law Society of Western Australia looking at ways the problems highlighted in the first report could be tackled.[9]

Many reports have also been generated in the United States on issues surrounding mental health and wellbeing in the legal profession. I will refer to some of the insights of these studies in other chapters. Perhaps matters are best summarised by Laura Rothstein, a professor of law at the University of Kansas, who said in her 2008 report on mental health and substance abuse problems amongst lawyers and law students, 'Although there is a great deal of research and information on these issues, *it is difficult to synthesise and assess what is working*' (my emphasis).[10]

Statistics, data, and percentages all have a way of inducing yawns and causing the eyes to glaze over. Stats can also be like a ventriloquist's dummy or case law – you can get them to say anything you like, as long as they agree with you. However, you may care to skim over the data cited above once again. One can reasonably be sceptical about one stat in isolation, but when such a volume of data all points in one direction, we should take particular notice. In this case, it seems clear that there is a serious and endemic problem in the legal profession. The solution? Well, that might not be so easy.

Wicked legal problems

In 1973 Horst Rittel and Melvin Webber, two professors at the University of California, published a seminal paper which introduced the idea of 'wicked problems' into the vocabulary to describe complex social problems to which there is no obvious solution.[11] In his 2012 book, Jon Kolko offers a useful definition of this term: 'A wicked problem is a social or cultural problem that is difficult or impossible to solve for as many as four reasons: incomplete or contradictory knowledge, the number of people and opinions involved, the large economic burden, and the interconnected nature of these problems with other problems'.[12]

I believe that the high incidence of mental illness in the legal profession can be regarded as a 'wicked legal problem'. To illustrate this, I will break down Kolko's description of wicked social problems and apply this to the legal profession.

Incomplete/contradictory knowledge

How to tackle mental illness in the legal profession is a problem which has attracted a great deal more attention in the UK and worldwide over the last decade. A number of thoughtful and thorough reports have been produced, some of which are mentioned above. Policy makers are now more informed. Wellbeing strategies are being thought out, and these have begun to be implemented in some of the larger law firms.

Reports are being considered and strategies tested, but the alarming statistics are clear evidence that practising lawyers and law students may be given technical competence in law, but to a significant degree, they may have limited awareness of the personal foundational skills which provide the basis for mentally healthy (and consequently competent) legal practice.

Number of people/opinions involved

Sometimes, however, the more information we have, the more complex the problem appears, and the more effort is required to tackle it. We can be overloaded and overwhelmed by data – it becomes difficult to see the wood from the trees. Studies have been undertaken by representatives of different branches of the legal profession (as described above). At times, lawyers regard themselves as colleagues of those in other branches of the profession, but at others competitors for different slices of the market. I suspect this may have something to do with sibling rivalry as well as self-protection. Any competitive element must to some extent undermine shared vision and motivation to work together. I will say a bit more about how groups can function and dis-function in Chapter 7.

Because of the vast amounts of information (and sometimes contradictory opinion) on this topic, it is difficult to know where to start. The answer to this question is always 'from here'.

The large economic burden

Addressing mental illness in the profession costs money, time, and effort. Up until recently, there was very little in the way of guidance as to how to consider the problem. In general, little or nothing is taught about mental wellbeing in law colleges and training institutions. Students are expected to have the necessary life skills to cope with what professional life throws at them.

There is no clear short-term financial gain for firms to address the issue. In view of this, costs targets and paying the bills inevitably take priority for the majority of law firms.

The interconnected nature of these problems with other social problems

Mental illness is a problem for society at large. It is clearly not limited to the legal or any other profession. It is said that one in four people in the UK will experience a mental health problem in the course of any year.[13] It is interesting that the one-in-four statistic correlates with approximately the same proportion of barristers experiencing almost intolerable stress levels. This may be purely co-incidental, but it may also be a warning bell.

For some, the illness is minor and transient; for others, deep-rooted and lifelong. Lawyers are not exempt from this. We are people. 400 years ago, Shakespeare's Dick the Butcher said,

'... the first thing we do, let's kill all the lawyers'. Attitudes to lawyers have not changed greatly. Despite public perception, stereotype, and urban myth, lawyers *are* human.

Stigma

Mixed in with the professional and social aspects of the problem is the huge problem of stigma. If anything, this is probably the most significant hindrance to thinking about and actually addressing the problem of mental health and wellbeing in the profession. Although a current motto for mental health awareness is 'no health without mental health', much of the time, little more than lip service is paid to this aspiration.

A stigma is a mark or brand that is seen by others and has much to do with how we feel we are perceived. On top of the stresses, pressures, and troubles that many people experience, stigma clouds the problem with thoughts of losing face, reduction in status, being seen as weak, fears of being overlooked for promotion, and worries about being perceived as fragile. It can lead to social isolation, exclusion, bullying, and scapegoating. Self-esteem is brought into the spotlight. We might fear a record of depression going onto our medical history and then having to declare this in the future in, for example, insurance proposals. A lawyer recently observed, 'It would be easier at work for me to come out as gay, than to ask for two weeks off for stress'.

As individuals, it may be that one of the biggest hurdles to overcome is facing the possibility that mental ill health might actually affect *me*, rather than the person working at the next desk.

Stress has had a bad press

The engineering formula for stress (stress = force/area), can be helpful in thinking about psychological stress. If we are subjected to an excessive overload of demands for a long period of time, then the pressure mounts and eventually something will give. Think of a stiletto shoe: weight is put on the sole and the heel of the shoe; it's the heel that penetrates grass. Or cutting butter with a knife; you can't do it with the flat of the knife.

After a period of extended pressure, we may begin to experience headaches, muscle tension or pain, exhaustion, upset stomach, sleep problems, chest pain; and mood changes such as general anxiety, lack of motivation, irritability, anger, sadness, or depression. These can also be precipitated by a trauma that is experienced briefly, but is sufficiently shocking to put us off balance.

In part because of the stigma associated with mental illness, it is far easier to say to someone that we feel 'stressed' and 'under pressure' rather than to say that we feel anxious, depressed, or that we have been self-medicating excessively. It is easier to use the convenient euphemism 'stress' as a blanket term for other stigmatising experiences that we would prefer not to articulate. When we talk about psychological stress, we are generally referring to a state of emotional or mental tension or strain resulting from adverse or very demanding circumstances. Stress is not a mental illness.

A doctor might write a sick note giving the reason for absence as 'stress', rather than 'anxiety' or 'depression', to help the patient present it to an employer. As I write, I will use the term 'stress' in this conventional sense, but also recognising that it is a general cover-all term for a variety of common psychological illnesses.

The American Bar Association undertakes a regular comprehensive survey of its lawyer assistance programmes. The 2014 survey showed that depression accounted for 50 per cent of lawyers' mental health impairments. Anxiety disorders accounted for 21 per cent. Other illnesses listed included addictions, personality disorders, obsessive compulsive disorder, grief, eating disorders, suicide attempts or ideation, ADHD, bipolar disorder, and dementia.[14] If the American data equates approximately to UK experience, what we are generally talking about when we talk about 'stress' is usually anxiety and depression.

In Figure 1, you will see a four-coloured stress ball. It illustrates the progression of stress in our own experience.

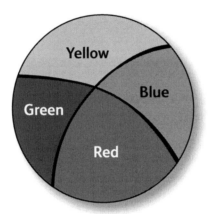

Figure 1: Stress sequence

The illustration is oversimplified, but may help to illustrate a complex dynamic:

- **The yellow zone** represents insufficient pressure, which can lead to boredom, rigidity, monotony, clock-watching, or '*under-stress*';

- **The green zone** represents appropriate pressure, which brings with it the opportunity of creativity, aliveness, productivity, profitability, resilience, and '*prehab*' (the next chapter explains the idea of prehab);

- **The red zone** represents excessive pressure leading to high anxiety, exhaustion, irritability, self-medication through alcohol or drugs, breakdowns in relationships ('*over-stress*'); which leads to

- **The blue zone**, which represents the blues, burnout, depression, mental illness, the need for prescription medication, therapy, and '*rehab*'.

Stress is neutral. It is just the result of excessive pressure (or in some cases the lack of pressure, through say unemployment or illness) that can tip us into the need for rehab.

Can stress be healthy?

A number of studies have recently emphasised the benefits of living a 'stress-full' life. These studies tend to contradict received wisdom that assumes that stress is undesirable and should be eliminated from our experience as much as possible. It is important that we have strategies to manage excessive demands and we will look at this later; however, it is also vital to recognise that we thrive on and are strengthened by the pressures that we experience.

In 2013, Alia Crum and others produced the report 'Rethinking Stress: The Role of Mindsets in Determining the Stress Response'.[15] Following three studies that explored the role of mindset in the context of stress, they point out that for many years the spotlight has been on negative aspects of stress (such as detrimental health effects, loss of productivity, and depression). They argue that this interpretation may be well-intended, but that the result of such a perspective could be counter-effective.

The study indicates that if people were prepared instead to adopt a 'stress-is-enhancing' mindset, this might have positive consequences in improved health and work performance. This does not mean that we should seek out more pressure, but that we do not need to focus single-mindedly on reducing our stress. The bottom line is essentially a positive one: finding the enhancing aspects of stress may be in part a matter of changing one's attitude.

In 2012 Jamison and others showed that changing the way we think about our bodily responses can improve our psysiological and cognitive reactions to stressful events.[16] Individuals who are better able to reappraise situations so as to decrease their emotional impact show more adaptive emotional and physiological responses when provoked to anger. They found that participants in the study who were instructed to reappraise or 'rethink' arousal as functional exhibited increased perceptions of available resources, improved cardiovascular functioning, and less threat-related attentional bias. So, in line with research on emotion regulation and cognitive behavioural therapy (CBT), interpretations of one's bodily signals impact on how the body and mind respond to acute stress.

Keller and others concluded in 2012 that high amounts of stress, and the perception that stress impacts negatively on health, are associated with poor physical and mental health.[17] Individuals who perceive that stress affects their health *and* who report a large amount of stress have an increased risk of premature death, for example.

In 2014 Abelson and others concluded that brief intervention to shift focus from 'competitive self-promotion' to a goal orientation of 'helping others' can help alleviate psychosocial stresses.[18] This supports the potential for developing brief interventions as inoculation tools to reduce the impact of predictable stressors and lends support to growing evidence that compassion and altruistic goals can moderate the effects of stress.

Adjusting your frame of mind

The positive takeaways from these recent reports indicate that we can all play a significant part in the impact that external and internal pressures have on us if our attitudes to the pressures can be managed, moderated, regulated, and thought about. We can play a significant part in whether the pressure benefits or harms us.

An altruistic frame of mind can inoculate against mental illness. For some of us, this may be the simple activity of managing our clients' interests, looking after our teams, or, for the judiciary, caring for the process of justice and thinking empathically about those in the court, wherever they may be sitting. The recent evidence tends to indicate that nature can be affected by our capacity to nurture.

To achieve this we must be proactive. It won't happen on its own. To avoid rehab we have first to consider prehab.

References
1. Department of Health, *No Health Without Mental Health: A Cross-Government Mental Health Outcomes Strategy for People of All Ages*, 2011.

2. Fujiwara, D., and Dolan, P., *Valuing mental health: how a subjective wellbeing approach can show just how much it matters,* UKCP, London, 2014.

3. LawCare, 'LawCare's Stress in the Legal Profession Survey', 2012.

4. The Law Society, 'Health and wellbeing report 2014', 6 August 2015; available at: www.lawsociety.org.uk/policy-campaigns/research-trends/research-publications/health-and-wellbeing-report-2014/.

5. The Bar Council, 'Wellbeing at the Bar', April 2015.

6. Gilbert, P., 'A report on the wellbeing of in-house lawyers', LBC Wise Counsel, 2015.

7. Thomas, C., '2014 UK Judicial Attitude Survey: Report of findings covering salaried judges in England & Wales courts and UK Tribunals', The Judicial Institute of University College London, 2015.

8. Kelk, N. J., Luscombe, G. M., Medlow, S., and Hickie, I. B., 'Courting the Blues: Attitudes towards depression in Australian law students and lawyers', *BMRI Monograph 2009–1*, Brain & Mind Research Institute, Sydney, 2009.

9. Kendall, C., 'Report on Psychological Distress and Depression in the Legal Profession', The Law Society of Western Australia, 2011.

10. Rothstein, L., 'Law Students and Lawyers with Mental Health and Substance Abuse Problems: Protecting the Public and the Individual', *University of Pittsburgh Review, 69,* 2008, pp.530–565.

11. Rittel, H. W. J., and Webber, M. W., 'Dilemmas in a General Theory of Planning', *Policy Sciences, 4,* 1973, pp.155–169.

12. Kolko, J., *Wicked Problems: Problems Worth Solving,* Austin Center for Design, 2012.

13. McManus, S., Meltzer, H., Brugha, T. et al, *Adult psychiatric morbidity in England, 2007: Results of a household survey,* The NHS Information Centre, Leeds, 2009.

14. American Bar Association, '2014 Comprehensive Survey of Lawyer Assistance Programs', ABA, Chicago, 2015.

15. Crum, A. J., Salovey, P., and Achor, S., 'Rethinking Stress: The Role of Mindsets in Determining the Stress Response', *Journal of Personality and Social Psychology, 104,* 2013, pp.716–733.

16. Jamieson, J. P., Nock, M. K., and Mendes, W. B., 'Mind over Matter: Reappraising Arousal Improves Cardiovascular and Cognitive Responses to Stress', *J Exp Psychol Gen, 141,* 2012, pp.417–422.

17. Keller, A., Litzelman, K., Wisk, L. E., et al., 'Does the Perception that Stress Affects Health Matter? The Association with Health and Mortality', *Health Psychol., 31,* 2012, pp.677–684.

18. Abelson, J. L., Erickson, T. M., Mayer, S. E., et al, 'Brief cognitive intervention can modulate neuroendocrine stress responses to the Trier Social Stress Test: Buffering effects of a compassionate goal orientation', *Psychoneuroendocrinology, 44,* 2014, pp.60–70.

Chapter 2:
Prehab

'They tried to make me go to rehab but I said, "No, no, no".'

Amy Winehouse

A Goldilocks planet is one which falls within its star's habitable zone. The earth is in the sun's Goldilocks zone: not too hot, not too cold, but just right, and containing the conditions for life to flourish. 'Prehab' can keep us in the Goldilocks zone.

Rehabilitation provides the setting for recovery from illness, injury, or addiction. By contrast, the idea of prehabilitation, or 'prehab' for short, describes a programme of training leading to the development of healthy practices to enhance wellbeing and reduce the risk of injury. It puts us in the Goldilocks zone.

Prehab contexts

Amongst athletes 'prehabilitation' is practised to avoid physical rehabilitation for sports injuries. The practice of an effective programme can help elite athletes to avoid injury in training and competition.

Athletic prehabilitation is designed to prevent injuries caused by body imbalances. For example, if someone works the stomach muscles but neglects the lower back, this can cause an imbalance that can lead to injury. A hamstring injury usually occurs when sprinting or jumping. Quite often, the upper side of the hamstring receives the injury so a stretching plan that incorporates the top and the bottom of the hamstring connections is critical. From a bio-mechanical perspective, we require balanced prehab to reduce the risk of injury.

A recent article uses the picture of a see-saw to illustrate a working definition of 'wellbeing'.[1] The authors propose the idea of a 'set point' for wellbeing, a position of rest between the fluctuating pressures of 'challenges' and 'resources'. The see-saw represents the drive of an individual to return to a set-point and balance for wellbeing.

On one side of the see-saw sit the 'resources' for wellbeing (psychological, social, and physical); the other is weighted by 'challenges' to wellbeing (psychological, social, and physical). Wellbeing is positioned like a ball at the fulcrum, at the point of balance. The authors state, 'in essence, stable wellbeing is when individuals have the psychological, social and physical resources they need to meet a particular psychological, social and/or physical challenge. When individuals have more challenges than resources, the see-saw dips, along with their well-being, and vice versa'.

To my mind this illustration is helpful, but also two-dimensional. Maybe we should not just be looking for balance in our lives, but *integration* of different aspects of life – synthesis as well as equilibrium.

The stresses that we experience as lawyers are not simply physical, or caused by excessive workloads or long hours. They are also *intra*personal and *inter*personal. The way that we cope with stresses is significantly determined by the meaning that we attribute to them and by those whose demands we are attempting to meet. Much will depend on the way that we have coped with similar requirements in the past. The demands placed on a young assistant solicitor by their supervisor or client may echo the expectations of university professors, school teachers, or a parent. Expectations of oneself generally originate from those of significant others.

As lawyers, we can face many difficult situations: a city associate pulling another all-nighter; an overloaded conveyancer keeping too many plates spinning; a high street partner with pressures from the bank manager; a family barrister dealing with another tragic children case; or a coroner struggling to cope with gore and others' grief.

Prehab can help us prepare for the emotional demands professional practice throws our way. It can also help us to think of our own characteristics as individual lawyers. In some part, we live up to stereotypes and archetypes.

Archetypes

Uriah Heep, Lionel Hutz, Atticus Finch – what do they have in common? Four syllables each and, in ascending order of reliability, they are all fictional lawyers.

Lawyers are a disparate group. We legislate for and advise most of humanity. Justice is, or should be, universal. Lawyers come from every background imaginable and practice in all jurisdictions. Millions of laws regulate innumerable human activities. Lawyers are reviled and revered, in debateable proportion.

Clearly, there are aspects of our role that engender respect and trust. We are trained to know the rules, how they work, and how they can be interpreted in a client's favour. Certain characteristics are necessary to enable us to do this effectively.

Recognising that certain aspects of legal practice can be more or less competitive or collaborative, contentious or non-contentious, we have certain traits that help us to do our jobs well:

- A draftsman who is conscientious, perfectionist, thorough, and attends to detail will have an advantage over another who is not.

- A partner in a law firm who is resilient, independent, and self-reliant will have the edge over rivals.

- A fee-earner who is competitive, driven, ambitious, and who has high expectations of their own performance and behaviour is more likely to achieve that one who is not self-motivated.

- An advocate who is persuasive, sceptical, good in debate, and who has strong personal charisma is likely to win more often than others.

- Counsel who is good on paper will benefit from being analytical, intellectual, and cautious, able to see both sides of the argument and give balanced advice.

However, this is just one side of the coin. On the other, where these characteristics become closely woven into a lawyer's sense of identity, personal satisfaction, self-esteem, and relationships, they can play out in a less functional manner. Aspects that are constructive in a courtroom can be destructive if played out in a family setting. What is helpful becomes self-defeating. The functional can become dysfunctional.

If the lawyer is unable to 'come out of role', or if there is a general over-identification with his or her professional self, one who is intellectual and analytical in professional life can be emotionally detached at home. Expectations of others in the family can be driven by achievement, successful completion of tasks, and winning over losing, rather than emotional attachment. One's worth can be measured in terms of achieving, rather than in relating.

Lawrence Krieger, clinical professor of law at Florida State University College of Law, puts it like this: 'Thinking "like a lawyer" is fundamentally negative; it is critical, pessimistic, and depersonalizing. It is a damaging paradigm in law schools because it is usually conveyed, and understood, as a new and superior way of thinking, rather than *an important but strictly limited legal tool*'[2] (author's emphasis). In other words, we have to think like lawyers to 'do law', but if we carry this too far, thinking like a lawyer may not help us to 'do life'.

High expectations of oneself and being looked up to by clients and fellow professionals can develop into an unhealthy narcissism. And overly tough and resilient persona can be accompanied by independent self-reliance and reluctance to seek help from others when it is needed at appropriate times.

A recent study demonstrated that people with perfectionist concerns experience high levels of work-related burnout.[3] If I 'know best', I am unlikely to seek or welcome feedback on performance. Feedback involves criticism, however constructive, and this can feed self-criticism. We will look at this more in Chapter 5.

Rehab for VIPs

The Menninger Clinic in Houston runs a Professionals in Crisis Program (PIC) designed to 'minimise the dysfunctional impact of the patient's position, power, prestige, wealth, or knowledge on the treatment process'.[4] The clinic treats lawyers, physicians, and mental health professionals; business executives and entrepreneurs; professional athletes; artists; priests, rabbis, and ministers; amongst others. Treating high achieving, well-educated individuals described as 'very important persons' (VIPs) presents clinicians with unique challenges. Typically, when professionals reluctantly agree to engage in treatment, they will 'minimise their difficulties, rationalise even the most maladaptive and outrageous behaviour, and seek to control, manipulate, intimidate, denigrate, or seduce their treaters'. Many of the patterns of behaviour that impede effective use of treatment in VIPs are deteriorations or exaggerations of behaviours that have contributed to the VIPs gaining and sustaining their professional position. Necessary strengths and characteristics, such as those listed above, become dysfunctional and are used by resistant professionals to inhibit the goals of therapy.

PIC is unique in that it allows professionals adequate time to immerse themselves in a therapeutic community. Residents receive individual therapy, medication, management, and group therapy over a period of around six to eight weeks. The therapy can be seen as a progression through three stages: re-moralisation, remediation, and rehabilitation. 'Re-moralisation' has the goal of resolving the acute crisis and restoring hope. 'Remediation' involves the resolution of the symptoms of the presenting psychiatric condition or behaviour, and 'rehabilitation' involves the restoration of psychological capacity (particularly mentalization) underlying adaptive healthy patterns of coping, experiencing, and relating.

Thinking back to the illustration of the stress sequence in the last chapter, we can see the individuals will brought from the blue 'rehab' area through the yellow area (where they are temporarily removed from the pressures and vicissitudes of excessive stress in their professional lives), back to the green area where hope and creativity are restored in large part. When the professional then begins to tip into the red area, they can manage the stresses and strains of working life with greater self-awareness. (Have a look again at the illustration in Chapter 1.)

Reversing the therapy

Prehab involves mentalizing and then putting into practice adaptive and healthy patterns of coping, experiencing, and relating, so that the risk of tipping into unhealthy symptomatology is minimised and life can be led with a sense of hope and morale. We will look at mentalizing in more detail in the next two parts of this book. The cycle of therapy is reversed: through prehab, the three stages of PIC therapy now become *pre*-moralisation, *pre*-mediation and *pre*-habilitation. It is about preventative psychology, being proactive as well as reactive.

Prehab training for athletes is essential for optimal performance. A limited training technique may cause tightness of muscle groups and imbalances of strength, coordination, or muscle stabilisation. Unnecessary and avoidable injury can side-line an athlete for months. Similarly, as lawyers we need not only the technical knowledge and skills to achieve to the best of our ability, but also (and equally importantly) the personal skills to do so in a way which facilitates and enhances performance. To do this, we need to think about ourselves, others, and what happens around us, and what we can do about it.

In the next parts of the book, we will look at these areas under the headings of 'Me', 'You', and 'Do' in turn.

References

1. Dodge, R., Daly, A. P., Huyton, J., and Sanders, L. D., 'The challenge of defining wellbeing', *International Journal of Wellbeing, 2 (3)*, 2012, pp.222–235.
2. Krieger, L. S., 'Institutional Denial About the Dark Side of Law School, and Fresh Empirical Guidance for Constructively Breaking the Silence', *Journal of Legal Education, 52*, 2002, pp.112–129.
3. Hill, A. P., and Curran, T. (in press), 'Multidimensional Perfectionism and Burnout: A Meta-Analysis', *Personality and Social Psychology Review.* Accepted for publication: June 2015.
4. Bleiberg, E., 'Treating Professionals in Crisis: A Mentalization-Based Specialized Inpatient Program'. In Allen, J. G., and Fonagy, P. (eds.), *Handbook of Mentalization-Based Treatment*, John Wiley & Sons, Chichester, 2006.

Part 2:
Me

The intra-personal *describes what goes on* within *our minds.*
It informs how we make sense of our thoughts, feelings, actions, and reactions through mindfulness.

Case study 1:
Andrew – Internalising problems

This case study is based on the experiences of one or more lawyers, which have been anonymised and rearranged for reasons of confidentiality. It illustrates several common pressures that can impact on lawyers' mental health, which are explored in more detail in the chapters that follow.

'It's like I never know when it's going to pounce.' 37-year-old criminal barrister Andrew was talking to his GP. Married with two young children and a growing practice, he had just been diagnosed with high blood pressure by his GP on a routine medical check-up. When his doctor asked him about his lifestyle, Andrew realised for the first time that things had been getting to be a bit much.

The demands of professional life and his own expectations of himself seemed to have grown over the last 10 years. He had worked most weekends over the last 18 months or so and was regularly working into the early hours during weekdays. He had recently lost an 'unlosable' case and had taken this badly. He was worried that the instructions from his solicitors might dry up. He had missed a crucial line of questioning in cross-examination and, although this probably did not affect the outcome of the trial, he was unable to shake it from his mind.

He realised that, at home, he had become more snappy and irritable with his wife and children. A glass of wine in the evening sometimes turned into a bottle, supplemented by strong coffee to help concentration in preparing for the next day in court. His sleep was poor, and he regularly woke around 4am, only to find himself running through the eventualities of the next day's case.

Although he had brushed it aside, he occasionally felt panicky when going to court, and on occasions recently had become lightheaded and had started sweating when he walked into the robing room. It seemed fine when he was on his feet, but sometimes in court he felt his thoughts scramble when his opponent was speaking. He experienced vague feelings of panic. When he thought about this, it seemed like there was a wild animal around somewhere. He identified feelings of edginess and discomfort. He said, 'I never know when it's going to pounce.'

His GP suggested that he could try relaxation exercises and recommended a CD of mindfulness breathing exercises. Andrew's initial response was sceptical, if not cynical. She also made some tactful suggestions about doing more exercise. Following a review, the GP prescribed medication to control his blood pressure, which at the time felt like a life sentence. 'I'm going to have to put these things down my bloody throat every day for the rest of my life.' An unwelcome reminder of mortality.

Andrew tried the relaxation exercises. His initial reaction was one of feeling foolish and rather pathetic. When he mentioned this in confidence to his head of chambers, the response was somewhat patronising: 'Well I suppose if I come into your room and see you sitting on your desk in the lotus position, at least I'll know what you're up to.'

He continued with the mindfulness exercises and gradually integrated them into his daily life. Whether it was the effect of the medication, or the breathing exercises, or a mixture of both, that reduced the sense of anxiety and panic, it did not really matter. For 15 minutes on the train on the way to work, he would just concentrate on his breathing. His mind often wandered. He gradually became more aware of what was happening inside and around him. After several months, he was able to recognise a growing sense of feeling grounded and safe.

As he went through the security scanner at court he would do a quick self-scan to identify if he was experiencing tension in any part of his body. In court, he gradually learned to regulate the feelings of panic by 'just listening to my breathing'. He also realised more clearly that he had been neglecting his family for his work and began to prioritise his time.

Few would have thought Andrew an anxious person. His clients, opponents, and the judiciary would have seen an independent and competent advocate. Behind this, however, he had learned to cope with vague feelings of anxiety through school, university, and his early professional life by simply getting on with things and ignoring the discomfort. After all, it was just part of how life was.

Chapter 3:
Brains and bodies

'A man's body and his mind, with the utmost reverence to both I speak it, are exactly like a jerkin and a jerkin's lining; rumple the one, you rumple the other.'

Laurence Sterne, *Tristram Shandy*

When we experience intolerable anxiety, our minds and bodies react in a variety of ways. We may feel overwhelmed, like we are losing control, become easily angered, irritable, and frustrated. We might begin to feel bad about ourselves.

Physically, we can also experience unpleasant symptoms. We may be troubled by headaches, stomach pains, nausea, chest pain, or rapid heartbeat. We can develop unexpected aches and pains. We might experience sweating, a dry mouth, or difficulty swallowing. Sometimes, people are unaware that they are clenching their jaws and grinding their teeth, perhaps in sleep. Insomnia can be common. We become more prone to frequent colds and infections. Libido can diminish, and we may be constantly tired and lacking in energy.

Socially, we can become difficult to live with. Sometimes, we become snappy and temperamental; at others, we may withdraw socially and find it easier to hide away. Sometimes, people around us will notice our anxieties and realise that maybe something is wrong.

Commonly, lawyers will carry on as normal and do their best to contain uncomfortable emotions. We are used to keeping a stiff upper lip. In order to look after our clients, we need to appear unruffled and capable; any sign of weakness could be seen as a chink in the armour and might work to our professional or tactical disadvantage.

Andrew in the case study kept things to himself. The pressure built up until he was forced to admit, after some probing by the GP, that things were not as he would wish them. In addition to the physical discomfort, what troubled him more was the loss of the sense of control both emotionally and in his thinking. He was alarmed when he experienced his 'thoughts scrambling' in court.

The cognitive changes that are brought about by cerebral processes in situations of extreme stress are remarkably complex and it is not the purpose of this book to go into detail about the subtleties of neurology. However, it is worth considering, at least superficially, how our brains react in stressful situations as it helps to explain why stress may be useful in some circumstances, and completely disabling in others.

Part of the neurological sequence goes something like this: Neuromodulator hormones are released in the peripheral and central nervous system during stress. These 'turn on' our heart and muscles and 'turn off' the stomach to prepare for flight or fight responses. At the same time, the brain may turn on a structure called the amygdala and then turn off the prefrontal cortex (a higher cognitive centre). This allows posterior cortical and subcortical structures to control our behaviour. The amygdala is known to be central for the expression of emotion and the formation of associations between stimuli and emotions.

The prefrontal cortex inhibits inappropriate responses or distractions and allows us to plan and organise effectively. High levels of the neuromodulators exert opposite actions on these brain regions.

Stimulation during periods of stress activates the amygdala and improves memory consolidation. During stress, the amygdala also induces increased hormone release in the prefrontal cortex. However, in contrast to the facilitative actions in subcortical structures, high levels of hormonal release in the prefrontal cortex results in cognitive dysfunction.

Exposure to mild-to-moderate uncontrollable stress impairs prefrontal cortical function. Sometimes, a person then feels they have no control over the stress. Simple routine functions can be performed quite satisfactorily, but anything requiring complex thought and imagination becomes difficult or impossible.[1]

Low and high roads to fear

Joseph LeDoux, professor of science at New York University, has written extensively on the phenomena of emotion and its function in the brain. He summarises the complex neural interactions that we experience in anxiety as follows (paraphrased):

Information about external stimuli reaches the amygdala by way of direct pathways from the thalamus (the low road) as well as by way of pathways from the thalamus to the cortex and then to the amygdala (the high road). The direct path from the thalamus to the amygdala is a shorter and faster transmission route than the path from the thalamus through the cortex to the amygdala. However, because the direct pathway bypasses the cortex, it is unable to benefit from cortical processing. As a result, it can only provide the amygdala with a crude

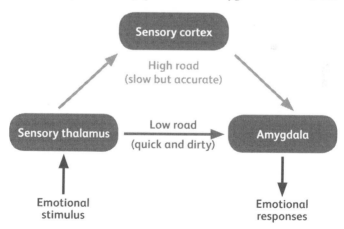

Figure 1: The low and high roads to fear

representation of the stimulus. It is what LeDoux terms a 'quick and dirty' processing pathway (see Figure 1). The direct pathway allows us to begin to respond to potentially dangerous stimuli before we fully know what the stimulus is. This can be very useful in dangerous situations. It is possible that the direct pathway is responsible for the control of emotional responses that we don't understand. This will occur in all of us some of the time, but it may be a predominant mode of functioning in individuals with certain emotional disorders.[2]

These two ways of reacting to stress can be both useful and 'unuseful', enabling and disabling. If I am in immediate physical danger, then the instinctive flight or fight response will help me to survive or avoid harm. However, it does not help when there is no actual physical danger and I need my prefrontal cortex to regulate appropriate thinking and acting. As an illustration, contrast the situation described below where I was confronted by a grizzly bear – a physical threat – and Andrew's response to walking into court, where there was no real danger.

The brain's survival mode

Some time ago, I was walking with friends in open ground above the tree line in the Canadian Rockies. Two of us were walking ahead of the others and we heard squeaking alarm calls from ground squirrels. We thought little of this and carried on walking. We stopped abruptly when we heard a shout from behind. About 50 yards ahead of us, crossing the path, was a mother grizzly with two cubs. We had not seen them because, from our viewpoint, they were just below a ridge. We froze. No way forward. And if we had tried to retreat we could quickly have been outrun. Thankfully, we were just far enough from the animals not to represent a threat to the cubs and they lumbered across the path and up the mountainside.

Now, here is the same scene in neurological terms: My thalamus received auditory and visual stimuli, which were shunted to the amygdala and the visual and auditory cortices. The amygdala registered a danger. It then triggered a fast physical reaction, to freeze. And when we saw the animals on the path, a clear image was sent to my conscious brain for a considered response: to freeze. The neural responses went from the sensory thalamus to the amygdala and on the 'quick and dirty' route. As a result, we stopped walking. Contemporaneously, as my friend and I assessed the situation in a split second, we were able to process what was going on, consider our options, and make a decision. We were probably also helped by the presence of another person to regulate our thinking. The stimulus also went from the sensory thalamus via the sensory cortex to the amygdala for processing an appropriate response.

We were able to use a system of 'functional' alarm. In contrast, Andrew, with his uncomfortable experience in court, was experiencing a 'false' alarm. Because of his earlier difficulties, generalised anxiety when younger, and a recent mishap in court which he experienced as devastating, levels of anxiety arose to such an extent that in court, as he was listening to his opponent's arguments and cross-examination, the stimulus took the low road and his thinking went off-line. In other words, he was unable to think about his thinking. He was unable to mentalize. In Andrew's words, his mind was 'scrambled'.

Jon Allen of the Menninger Clinic puts it like this: 'Stress is the enemy of mentalization; when anxiety reaches a certain level the mentalizing brain goes offline and moves into survival-mode.'[3] We look at the idea of mentalization in Chapter 5.

The 'high road' to clearer thinking

Daniel Siegel, professor of clinical psychiatry at the University of California, Los Angeles, has illustrated the process of the anxiety response with the example of the hand.[4] It goes something like this: Hold your open hand in front of you, looking at the palm. Fold your thumb across the palm of your hand and then fold the four fingers over the thumb. Your wrist and palm represent the brainstem, responsible for survival instincts (automatic functions). The thumb represents the midbrain where we store and integrate memories and hold fears. The fingers over the thumb represent the cortex which processes perception, motor action, speech, and what we normally call 'thinking'.

The fingernails represent the prefrontal cortex (approximately behind the eyes), a primary integration centre for the brain. This is responsible for various functions such as regulation of the body through the autonomic nervous system, emotional regulation, management of interpersonal relationships, response flexibility, intuition, self-awareness, and morality. When we are stressed or overwhelmed the prefrontal cortex shuts down temporarily. Thinking is 'scrambled'.

Now, lift the fingers from the palm of your hand so that the thumb is exposed. This illustrates the removal of the prefrontal cortex from the process. The 'high' road through the prefrontal cortex is blocked off and the stimuli are now going straight from the sensory thalamus to the amygdala along the quick-and-dirty 'low road'. Higher functioning coping strategies such as anticipation, altruism, humour, self-assertion, and self-observation are deactivated.

The trick is to keep on thinking and keep on the high road as much as possible. But how? This might all seem rather fatalistic if there is nothing we can do about the situation. However, there are steps we can take, and part of the answer is through gaining resilience by mentalizing. We will address resilience in the next chapter.

References

1. Arnsten, A. F. T., 'Neuroscience: The Biology of Being Frazzled', *Science, 280*, 1998, pp.1711–1712.
2. LeDoux, J., *The Emotional Brain: The Mysterious Underpinnings of Emotional Life*, Simon & Schuster, New York, 1996.
3. Allen, J. G., and Fonagy, P., *Handbook of Mentalization-Based Treatment*, John Wiley & Sons Ltd., Chichester, 2006.
4. Siegel, D. J., and Hartzell, M., *Parenting from the Inside Out*, Penguin Putnam, New York, 2003.

Chapter 4:
Resilience

*'This is how sailors' bodies are hard-
ened against the sea, farmers' hands are
calloused, soldiers' arms are strong enough
for throwing javelins, runners' legs are swift.
In each case, what is exercised the most
is the toughest.'*

Seneca, *Selected Dialogues and Consolations*

The devastation caused in New Orleans by Hurricane Katrina in 2005 may seem a world apart from the overwhelming situation facing a barrister in central London. One involves an environmental disaster affecting thousands of people over a wide area; the other, a local crisis facing one individual and having immediate implications for only a handful of others. However, the environmental disaster and Andrew's crisis have much in common.

Judith Rodin, president of the Rockefeller Foundation, and former president of the University of Pennsylvania, has written recently on the social implications of the destruction brought about by Katrina and by Superstorm Sandy in New York in 2012. She concludes that, without resilience, communities and individuals are unable to bounce back from crises, learn from them, and achieve revitalisation.[1]

Andrew faced a crisis. It came about through the combination of internal and external stresses that he found overwhelming, confusing, and impossible to manage. After receiving support from his GP, he was able to adopt a number of strategies to help him begin to get his life back on track. In Churchill's words, he 'did not let a good crisis go to waste'. The same principles, argues Rodin, apply to social groups on a global scale.

Resilience theory

Over the last decade, a large body of literature has been produced at academic and popular levels to apply theory in the area of resilience. Various definitions of the concept and scope of 'resilience' have been suggested. For example, resilience is 'an interactive concept that refers to a relative resistance to environmental risk experiences, or the overcoming of stress or adversity'.[2] Or, it is 'normal development under difficult conditions'.[3] It implies 'exposure to risk factors (adversities) and protective factors (beneficial resources) leading to developmentally appropriate (and thus resilient) outcomes'.[4]

A reasonable working definition was coined by Ian Dowie, the former manager of the London football club Crystal Palace: 'bouncebackability'. This gets closer to the original sense of the word which means to 'rebound' or 'recoil', implying the elasticity and toughness individuals and communities need to recover from personal and wider crises.

In our own experience, we will all have noted that, when confronted with a crisis, some people seem to cope better than others. This general impression is backed up by academic research into resilience, such as that of Michael Rutter, professor of developmental psychopathology at Kings College, London. Rutter's studies demonstrate that there is considerable variation in peoples' responses to various amounts of environmental adversity.[5] Negative experience may have either a 'sensitising' effect or a strengthening ('steeling') effect in relation to the response to later stress or adversity.

While some people may be more vulnerable than others to adverse pressure because of innate predisposition ('nature') or earlier life experiences ('nurture'), he also noted that an individual's ability to cope with adversity may be affected by 'turning point effects' associated with experiences that increase opportunities and enhance coping. A strong, supportive adult relationship, for example, can effect a turning point and can have a significant beneficial effect on our ability to cope.[6] This may be from a partner, friend, a work colleague, mentor, LawCare volunteer, or therapist. The indication is that where an individual feels safe and has positive relationships, they are more able to rise above adversity and to think more clearly about their own and others' mental states; in other words, to mentalize. Because it enables more flexible and objective thinking, mentalizing can protect self-esteem and self-efficacy. Even when someone is more vulnerable than others to the negative effects of stress through prior difficulty, this capacity can be developed in close relationships at any point in life.

One broad thrust from this research is that significant amounts of adversity can actually predispose us to better outcomes when facing later difficulties. This flies in the face of much popular current theory about stress reduction and avoidance of stress, but it probably reflects much of our own experience as lawyers: we would not have got to where we are in our profession, whether a trainee, associate, head of chambers, or senior judge, had we not built up a certain resilience over long hours and steady pressure from law school on. It looks like Seneca was on the right lines when he said that 'what is exercised the most is the toughest'.

Research carried out in the field of child development also suggests that certain characteristics may determine how individuals cope with stress. According to the research, characteristics that appear to protect children from the adverse effects of stressful experience include high intelligence and good problem-solving ability, effective coping styles, autonomy, a sense of self-worth, interpersonal awareness and empathy, planning abilities, and a sense of humour.[7]

Anecdotally, a number of these qualities are reflected in psychiatric literature. In the fourth version of the *Diagnostic and Statistical Manual of Mental Disorders* of the American Psychiatric Association (DSM-IV) effective coping styles are listed including anticipation, affiliation, altruism, humour, self-assertion, self-observation, sublimation, and suppression.[8] We will look at these in more detail in Chapter 9 and explore how they can be applied to our day-to-day experiences at work and at home.

An optimistic conclusion to all of this is that we can learn to develop these qualities in the context of supportive relationships to boost our 'psychological immune system'.[9] To this end, the American military is currently in the process of adopting a model of resilience training, developed by Martin Seligman and others, to build mental toughness under the title of 'Master Resilience Training'.[10] The programme is not without its critics, but it appears to have been adopted and accepted widely in a stereotypically macho culture. Seligman admits that he and his colleagues were nervous that hard-boiled soldiers would find resilience training 'touchy-feely' or 'psychobabble'. Contrary to expectation, the general response has been particularly favourable.

The programme incorporates training from various therapeutic approaches. For example, the mental toughness segment uses a cognitive model derived from Albert Ellis's ABCD model: soldiers are shown that emotional Consequences stem not from Adversity but from one's Beliefs about adversity, leading to an ability to effectively Dispel unrealistic beliefs about adversity. It examines thinking traps such as overgeneralising and catastrophic thinking, and challenges 'icebergs' – deeply held beliefs such as 'asking for help is a sign of weakness'. There is an emphasis on positive communication in military teams and encouragement to build on signature strengths of the group.

The idea of resilience can be applied at an individual and an institutional level. For example, at the individual level we have a *lawyer*, the *group* in which he or she works (a set of chambers, a team within a larger organisation, a law firm), and the wider legal *community* (which would include other firms or chambers, clients, professional bodies, and the court system). One could also look at these groupings and consider their own qualities of resilience. This is beyond the scope of this short book and

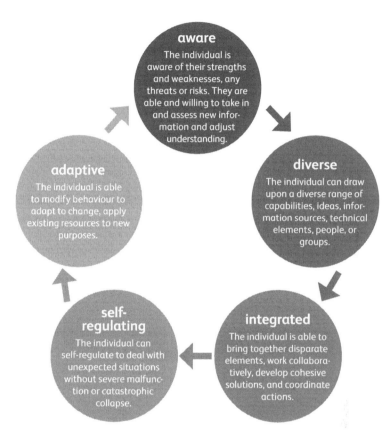

Figure 1: Rodin's five characteristics of resilience

we will limit ourselves to considering personal and individual resilience. The principles, however, can be extrapolated.

Resilience markers

Rodin outlines five characteristics of resilience; namely, awareness, diversity, integration, the capacity for self-regulation, and adaptability (see Figure 1).[11] An individual or a community needs all five to be resilient, she argues. Sometimes threats experienced or perceived by an individual can seem innumerable, but analysing them in the light of these five principles can aid clarification. To illustrate, we will look at the five principles in the light of Andrew's experience.

Aware
An individual needs to be *self*-aware and *situationally* aware. It is rather like doing one's own personal SWOT analysis. We look at our own strengths and assets, liabilities and vulnerabilities, and any threats or risks that we are exposed to. We think about our own resources realistically, and also about the situations that we face. The process is dynamic and fluid. We constantly assess and reassess, taking in new information when circumstances change.

Andrew's capacity for awareness was significantly limited by his physical exhaustion through overwork, his high self-expectation, feelings that he would be judged by his instructing solicitor, a fear that his perceived failure in court would lead to significant financial difficulties, a loss of emotional warmth given to and received from his family, and increasing unrecognised general and specific anxiety which had begun to show itself in latent physical symptoms. His lack of awareness inhibited his perception of the physical discomfort that he was experiencing and what this might be leading to. This led to a lack of situational awareness and an unrealistic appraisal of the consequences of his own sense that he had let himself and his client down in court. His anxiety overrode his thinking. In other words, in quasi-neurological terms, his brain took the 'low road', rather than the 'high road' (see Chapter 3).

Diverse
An entity needs to be diverse and have different sources of capacity so that it can successfully operate when some elements of capacity are challenged. We must be able to draw from a range of capabilities, ideas, information sources, technical elements, people, or groups. Again, anxiety inhibited Andrew's

competence in drawing from other resources. He tried to obtain support from his head of chambers but was sceptically rebuffed, or at least that is how he perceived it. Others would have seen him as competent in many aspects of life, but because of his increasing tunnel vision and inability to think about himself realistically (in other words to mentalize), he was restricted in his ability to draw from other resources.

Integrated

A resilient person requires integration, in other words a coordination of functions and actions, including the ability to bring together disparate elements, and work collaboratively to develop cohesive solutions and coordinate actions. Andrew was unable to think realistically about his other strengths and abilities and to see that one or two minor errors, to which everyone is prone, even the perfectionist, did not mean that he could not be sufficiently competent overall and both give a good account of himself and represent his client effectively.

Self-regulating

He was unable to self-regulate. He began to experience panic in court. Self-regulation contains the idea of a system 'failing safely'. He was unable to modulate his response and experienced a relatively minor failing as disastrous. Catastrophic thinking followed.

Adaptive

His behaviour and thinking about himself became rigid and unimaginative. Panic ensued and anxiety inhibited the ability to improvise and be flexible. It also prevented him from thinking about himself in a kindly way rather than self-judgementally.

A turning point

As we saw, things changed and Andrew's ability and competence in self-awareness, drawing from other resources, integrating and coordinating his responses, self-regulation and flexibility, changed gradually, in the main with the support of his GP. He reached a 'turning point'. He began to be able to 'think about his thinking' in a more realistic and effective way.

What were some of the factors that helped Andrew to move to becoming more resilient? And why did some simple life adjustments help him to turn the corner?

This had something to do with mindfulness.

References

1. Rodin, J., *The Resilience Dividend: Managing disruption, avoiding disaster, and growing stronger in an unpredictable world*, Profile Books, London, 2015.
2. Rutter, M., 'Implications of Resilience Concepts for Scientific Understanding', *Annals New York Academy of Sciences, 1094*, 2006, pp.1–12.
3. Fonagy, P., Steele, M., Steele, H., et al, 'The Emmanuel Miller Memorial Lecture 1992: The theory and practice of resilience', *Child Psychology & Psychiatry & Allied Disciplines, 35*, 1994, pp.231–257.
4. Stein, H., 'Does Mentalizing Promote Resilience?' In Allen, J. G., and Fonagy, P. (eds.), *Handbook of Mentalization-Based Treatment*, John Wiley & Sons, Chichester, 2006.
5. Rutter, M., 'Resilience as a dynamic concept', *Development and Psychopathology, 24*, 2012, pp.335–344.
6. Stein *supra* note 4.
7. Fonagy, P., Steele, M., Steele, H., et al, *supra* note 3.
8. American Psychiatric Association, *Diagnostic and Statistical Manual of Mental Disorders – Text revision (4th ed.)*, American Psychiatric Association Press, Washington, 2000.
9. Holmes, J., *The search for the secure base: Attachment theory and psychotherapy*, Routledge, Hove, 2001.
10. Seligman, M. E. P., 'Building Resilience', *Harvard Business Review, 89*, 2011, pp.100–108.
11. Rodin *supra* note 1.

Chapter 5:
Practical mentalizing (1) – Mindfulness

'Know thyself.'

Delphic maxim

A CIA interrogation manual from the mid-1960s admitted that 'regression' in the psychic sense is the aim of interrogation. The anonymous author wrote that it was necessary to 'obliterate the familiar and replace it with the weird'. He called it 'the Alice in Wonderland or confusion technique', and the object was 'to confound the expectations and conditioned reactions of the interrogatee. He is accustomed to a world that makes some sense, at least to him: a world of continuity and logic, a predictable world'.[1]

Under extreme stress, we can lose touch with what is familiar, logical, and predictable, and experience confusion and loss of control. Andrew experienced feelings of panic in the courtroom. His confidence was undermined and he began to feel, without any rational justification, that he was not up to the task in hand. It was as if his high expectations of himself had assumed an exaggerated and oppressively demanding quality. He had a vague sense that his thinking was unrealistic, yet was unable to rein in the anxiety.

Many people have written of the demanding nature of an inner critical voice. Sigmund Freud speculated about a three-part personality: the ego, superego, and id (literally, 'I', 'Over-I', and 'It'). For Freud, the superego represented the ethical component of personality, providing the individual with moral standards, inherited in the main from parental figures. Often, the inner parent could be harsh and punitive: 'one part of the ego (the superego) sets itself against the other (the ego, or conscious self), judges it critically, and, as it were takes it as its object'.[2]

However we term it, Andrew's punitive and harsh inner critic, fed by his anxiety, inhibited his ability to see what was happening in court in a realistic way and distorted his ability to mentalize. It was as if his thinking had gone off-line, switched off by anxiety.

Psychiatrist David Malan proposed a simple model of the workings of anxiety and how we instinctively try to manage it (see Figure 1). His model of a 'triangle of conflict' consists of defence (D), anxiety (A), and hidden feeling (HF). Anxieties are experienced in the context of human relationships. The triangle stands on one apex (hidden feeling), representing the fact that the aim of most dynamic psychotherapy is to reach beneath the defence and the anxiety to the hidden feeling, and then to trace this feeling back from the present to its origins in the past. Often, this relates to parents or parental figures.[3]

A simple analysis of the triangle in Andrew's situation might be that he was experiencing anxiety from fear of failure,

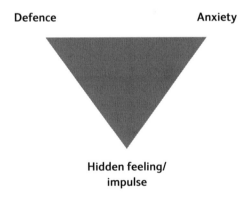

Defence   **Anxiety**

**Hidden feeling/
impulse**

Figure 1: Malan's Triangle of Conflict

financial loss, loss of reputation, and personal humiliation. This might have been in the context of professional rivalry or comparisons that he drew between himself and others in his chambers. He would largely have been unaware of these hidden feelings. He attempted to defend himself against the anxiety by repression and denial (trying to ignore the physical discomfort that his anxiety was causing him), intellectualisation (trying to think his way through the difficulty), and alexithymia (an inability to read the emotions that he was experiencing). All of these 'defensive mechanisms' or 'coping strategies' were maladaptive. He was using them at the expense of his true health.

Had he been able to think more clearly and objectively and acknowledge what he was experiencing, he could have used more adaptive and realistic ways of coping, such as those outlined in the last chapter and in Chapter 9. The thinking part of his brain, principally the prefrontal cortex, would have been integrated and activated and he would have been able to obtain a more effective position of self-observation and consequently performance. In short, had he been able to mentalize more clearly, he would have been able to cope more effectively.

Mentalizing

'Mentalizing simply implies a focus on mental states in oneself or in others, particularly in explanations of behaviour. That mental states influence behaviour is beyond question. Beliefs, wishes, feelings and thoughts, whether inside or outside our awareness, determine what we do'.[4]

Mentalizing involves a capacity for interpretation of thoughts and actions, to 'think about thinking'. It is experiential in the sense of being a starting point for thinking. A thought is often accompanied by bodily sensations, emotions, and/or images. This is followed by an awareness or noticing what one is thinking and feeling. Then one is able to think about what one has caught oneself thinking about. If we think about our thinking, this is 'explicit' mentalizing. 'Implicit' mentalizing involves these processes, but we remain unaware of the act.

Mentalizing is concerned with the meanings that we attribute to our own and others' actions. It is a skill that can be present or absent to greater or lesser degrees.[5]

When considering the process of mentalizing in the context of relationships with other people, it incorporates other equivalent concepts such as 'mindblindness', empathy, and emotional intelligence. We will look at these in more detail in Chapter 6.

Mindfulness

When we are thinking about when an individual is involved in interpreting his or her own actions on the basis of intentional mental states (such as physical sensation, desires, needs, feelings, and the like), the related concept of 'mindfulness' is particularly helpful.

In the late 1980s, after a decade or so of research, Ellen Langer wrote her book *Mindfulness* as a way of translating the technical jargon of psychological research for a wider readership. She concluded that 'mindfulness and mindlessness are so common that few of us appreciate their importance or make use of their power to change our lives'.[6]

In a co-authored paper, Langer later defined mindfulness as 'the process of drawing novel distinctions. It does not matter whether what is noticed is important or trivial, as long as it is new to the viewer'. She says that actively drawing these distinctions is what keeps us situated in the present. This can lead to a greater sensitivity to one's environment, more openness to new information, the creation of new categories for structuring perception, and enhanced awareness of multiple perspectives in problem solving.[7]

Interestingly, in the same paper, she noted that perceived control had been shown to have very positive effects on stress reduction and health, and that when a person behaves mindlessly, the perception of control is not possible. This correlates exactly with the experience outlined above of people subjected to interrogation or torture, and indeed to Andrew's own experience of feeling out of control. She also highlighted that studies in the 1980s showed that increases in mindfulness were associated with increased creativity and productivity, and decreased psychological burnout.

The practice of mindfulness meditation – which has its origins in ancient Buddhist practices – has been shown to be effective in enhancing mental health and has been applied in treating mood disorders (anxiety, depression), intrusive thinking (ruminations, hallucinations, memories), behaviours (bingeing, addiction, self-harm, violence), problems of relating (attitudes, empathy) and problems related to oneself (self-consciousness, self-hatred).[8]

It has been shown to increase personal resilience, and it has been demonstrated that those participating in studies have reported feeling happier, more energised, and less stressed. They felt that they had far more control over their lives. Some also found that their lives had more meaning and that challenges could be seen as opportunities rather than threats.[9]

Mindfulness is the 'antithesis of mental habits in which the mind is on "automatic pilot". In this usual state, most experiences pass by completely unrecognised, and awareness is dominated by a stream of internal comment whose insensitivity to what is immediately present can seem mindless'.[10] Andrew's breathing exercises on the train on his way to work helped him, in part, to press the pause button and to create some space where he could learn to calm himself sufficiently to regain a sense of perspective and control over his working life. (Exercises designed to help you 'press pause' and reflect on what's going on inside and around you are included in Chapters 9 and 10.)

We have looked at the significance of a mindful approach which helps us to mentalize, to be more aware of what is going on *within* ourselves. We will now look at what happens *between* us and others.

References
1. Belton, N., *The Good Listener. Helen Bamber: A Life Against Cruelty*, Weidenfeld & Nicholson, London, 1998.

2. Freud, S., *Mourning and Melancholia, Standard Edition Volume 14*, Hogarth Press, London, 1917.

3. Malan, D. H., *Individual Psychotherapy and the Science of Psychodynamics*, Arnold, London, 2001.

4. Bateman, A. W., and Fonagy, P., *Mentalization-Based Treatment for Borderline Personality Disorder: A Practical Guide*, Oxford University Press, 2006.

5. Holmes, J., *The search for the secure base: Attachment theory and psychotherapy*, Routledge, Hove, 2001.

6. Langer, E. J., *Mindfulness*, Addison-Wesley, Reading, MA, 1989.

7. Langer, E. J., and Moldoveanu, M., 'The Construct of Mindfulness', *Journal of Social Issues, 56*, 1–9, 2000.

8. Mace, C., 'Mindfulness in psychotherapy: an introduction', *Advances in Psychiatric Treatment, 13*, 2007, pp.147–154.

9. Williams M., and Penman, D., *Mindfulness: a practical guide to finding peace in a frantic world*, Piatkus, London, 2011.

10. Mace, *supra* note 8.

Part 3:
You

The inter-personal *describes what goes on* between *minds when minds meet, both one-to-one and in groups. It informs how we make sense of others' thoughts, feelings, actions, and reactions through mind-mindedness.*

Case study 2:
Beth – Inter-personal causes of stress

This case study is based on the experiences of one or more lawyers, which have been anonymised and rearranged for reasons of confidentiality. It illustrates several common pressures that can impact on lawyers' mental health, which are explored in more detail in the chapters that follow.

It was pretty much out of desperation that Beth telephoned LawCare one lunchtime. She had been vaguely aware that there were some organisations which provided help for lawyers in difficulty. Following a Google search, she had found the LawCare website and downloaded some information about stress and bullying. When the phone was dialling, she could feel her heart pounding. It had taken a great effort to decide to call and, when a helpline lawyer answered the call, she felt rather tongue-tied. Gradually, she was able to tell her story and was almost overwhelmed by relief when she put the phone down almost an hour later.

Beth was 28. After graduating, she had joined a large city firm as a trainee. The firm had kept her on as an associate and she was spending long days as a young corporate lawyer. Over the last year the hours had increased, and the expectations of her profitability had grown. 15-hour days were becoming more common and although she was not really aware of it, she was becoming increasingly tired and had begun to make silly mistakes. Nothing serious, only arithmetical errors and clerical oversights; however, she was acutely aware of them and was increasingly beginning to feel that she had made the wrong career choice.

Four months previously, she had missed an important deadline on one of her files. Nothing turned on it and it caused no difficulty with the client, but her supervisor, Steve, made much of it. Not only did he lose his temper with her in private after it came to light, but he let everyone in their team know what had happened too. From then onwards, she felt that she would take the blame for any difficulties within the department. On occasions, Steve would say things which on their face could have been innocuous, but were clearly loaded and intended to humiliate her publicly.

The longer working hours meant that she was unable to go out with friends as much as she had in the past. She became increasingly socially isolated, stopped going to the gym, and felt that she had no one with whom she could share her worries. There seemed no way out, other than to hand in her resignation or apply for another job elsewhere. Moving would probably also mean a fair reduction in salary and she had worked out that this would mean downsizing her flat. She had thought about giving up the law entirely and maybe opening a coffee shop. She did not feel brave enough for this and all the financial uncertainty it would involve.

As her story unfolded, the LawCare helper's questions made her think of things that had not occurred to her before. Was it possible the long hours might be having some effect on the mistakes that she was making? Had she raised the issue of her colleague's bullying with his superior? Did she feel able to raise the bullying issue directly with the supervisor? Was she working the long hours purely to meet the time recording requirements of the firm, or also to impress people? They looked at the options of staying with the same firm, moving to another firm in the same area, and moving location. They thought in general about the possibility of leaving the law. The helper made a number of suggestions about ways in which she could think about her position. As a result, she googled 'transactional analysis' and was helped by the insight that people can unconsciously adopt parent, adult, and child roles in relationships.

The helper wondered whether Beth might like some free ongoing support from a LawCare volunteer who had experienced similar problems to hers. She was put in touch with another lawyer with whom she talked on the phone at prearranged times over the next three months or so. Together, they were able to think about what was happening in the workplace and to plan ways in which she could find her voice, particularly with her difficult supervisor. She had been on the point of making a complaint about her supervisor, but things settled down after she plucked up the courage to talk to him in a more self-assertive way about how he was behaving.

After this talk, she was able to understand a bit more about the pressures he was under. She thought this might have been fuelling some of his aggression towards her. She became more disciplined in her timekeeping and prioritised regular times for meeting friends. After the talk with Steve, she realised more clearly that others in the department had also felt intimidated by him and that she had not been the only one. She had not been able to see it that way previously.

After the involvement with the LawCare volunteer finished, Beth was weighing up her options of staying with the firm or applying for work elsewhere.

Chapter 6:
Practical mentalizing (2)
– Mind-mindedness

'If you can learn a simple trick, Scout, you'll
get along a lot better with all kinds of folks.
You never really understand a person until
you consider things from his point of view
– until you climb into his skin and walk
around in it.' (Atticus Finch)

Harper Lee, *To Kill a Mockingbird*

How is it that some people seem to breeze through life effortlessly? What secret do they have that enables them to ride pressures and demands? Sometimes, from the outside, it seems that other people's lives are simple and easy. We know that this is far from reality, but sometimes it does not seem so.

Around one in four people in the UK will experience some form of clinically recognisable mental illness within the course of a year.[1] On the face of it, the statistic is alarming and almost incredible. What is certain is that, if we accept this as true, lawyers will not be exempt. Moreover, for all of us who see others as calm, confident, and competent (in contrast to ourselves), this statistic shows that what is on the surface does not necessarily reflect what is happening inside (as the previously cited example of Andrew illustrates).

Something is not working for the 25 per cent, but conversely, the maths indicate that something *is* working for the 75 per cent. So, what makes the difference? By and large, it may be rooted in childhood experience.

Working with war orphans in London in the 1940s and

1950s, psychiatrist John Bowlby developed his theories of human attachment, controversial with the psychoanalytic community at the time. From this work, Bowlby and others proposed that the basic, motivating force for human beings was the drive for connection. We seek contact with, love and support from, engagement with, and encouragement from other people. Many war orphans, robbed of the nurture, example, and direction of parents, demonstrated alarming ways of dealing with this lack. Similarly, when adults find themselves unable to cope with excessive pressures, it may be that they lack (temporarily, perhaps because they are too busy at work) the secure base represented by relationships with family and friends, which can help them to cope.

Bowlby noted that some children became socially isolated and withdrawn. Their instinctive way of dealing with human relationships when they went wrong or when they experienced conflict, was to internalise the anxiety and deal with it on their own, essentially shunning any help that was on offer. Conversely, others reacted by becoming excessively clingy to their caregivers. The terms 'avoidant' and 'ambivalent' were used to describe these two contrasting ways of coping, both of which were considered by Bowlby to be 'insecure' forms of attachment.

By contrast, Bowlby's term a 'secure base' summarised his concept of healthy attachment.[2] Without this, an individual lacks the capacity to integrate experience and relate to others adequately. The psychoanalyst Donald Winnicott said (using the word symbolically to signify 'caregiver'), that the mother only needs to be 'good enough'. In other words, childhood experience does not have to be perfect. Indeed, for resilience to develop, the child and growing adult must be exercised by experience, but to a degree that is proportionate with their ability to cope. The maintenance of a good supportive environment, a 'secure base', is primarily the task of the child's caregivers who will moderate adverse experience.

Within the environment of the secure base, the child learns to relate to others, recognise what others may be thinking and feeling, and gradually to develop a sense of empathy. Within this environment they learn to mentalize. They learn to interpret what other people do or say as meaningful and that others' motivation is informed by their feelings, beliefs, reasons, thoughts, stresses, needs, or desires.

Without this learned competence, without the security of an internal secure base, the child will experience life as confusing and chaotic. They will then respond to stresses 'avoidantly', withdrawing within themselves and try to sort life out on their own (much as we saw with Andrew) or 'ambivalently', reaching out to others for security and support which they feel they lack in themselves. Broadly speaking, the latter was Beth's instinctive way of dealing with difficulties in the workplace and before receiving the help and support from LawCare. Generally one to rely on support from friends and family, she was unable to do so at a time of exhaustion and overwork. For both, their ways of relating and seeking help were not 'good enough'.

Thinking feelings and feeling thinkings

In 1909, Edward Titchener introduced a new word in the English language: 'empathy'. The word literally means 'in-feeling'. We generally use it to describe an ability to understand and appreciate another person's feelings or experience.

Before we can imagine what others may be feeling, we first have to be able to identify our own emotions. For many this is difficult. For Andrew it was almost impossible. In psychotherapy, identifying and labelling one's feelings is sometimes one of the hardest things to do.

Peter Fonagy, Freud Memorial Professor of Psychoanalysis at University College London, introduced the concept of 'mentalized affectivity' to refer to a skill that that we all need, the ability to mentalize emotionally, that is to feel and think about our feelings at the same time.[3] This requires a comfort and familiarity with our own emotions. 'Emotions relate directly to our achievement of, or failure to achieve, specific wishes or desires'.[4]

Beliefs about having achieved goals or desires will inevitably generate an emotional response.

Emotional intelligence

Popularised by science journalist Daniel Goleman in the 1990s, the concept of 'emotional intelligence' was developed by psychology professors John Maher and Peter Salovey in the United States. In 1990 Maher and Salovey published a paper presenting a framework for emotional intelligence, a set of skills hypothesised to contribute to the accurate appraisal and expression of emotion in oneself and in others, the effective regulation of emotion in self and others, and the use of feelings to motivate and achieve in one's life.[5]

14 years later, Mayer and Salovey, with colleague David Caruso, published findings on research into emotional intelligence. They defined 'emotional intelligence' as 'the capacity to reason about emotions, and of emotions to enhance thinking'. It includes the ability to accurately perceive emotions, to access and generate emotions so as to assist thought, to understand emotions and emotional knowledge, and to reflectively regulate emotions so as to promote emotional and intellectual growth.[6]

They proposed a four branch ability model to clarify emotional intelligence:

- Branch one reflects the *perception* of emotion and involves the capacity to recognise emotions in others' facial and postural expressions;

- Branch two, *facilitation*, involves the capacity of emotions to assist thinking;

- The third branch, the *understanding* of emotion, reflects the capacity to analyse emotions, appreciate their probable trends over time, and understand their outcomes; and

- Branch four reflects the *management* of emotion, which necessarily involves the rest of the personality.

Much has been written in popular psychological and management literature about the practical application of emotional intelligence. Goleman and others have written at length on its application to enhance ones' own and one's business life. We have seen how Beth, with the support of the LawCare helper (and without knowing the theory), began to use emotional intelligence in her dealings with Steve.

Mindblindness and mind-mindedness

At around the same time that Mayer and Salovey were writing, in the UK Simon Baron-Cohen and others at the Autism Research Centre at Cambridge University were working on producing the first electronic encyclopaedia of emotions. A DVD was produced entitled 'Mind Reading: the interactive guide to emotions'.[7] The work was motivated by the lack of any tailor-made educational software for people on the autistic spectrum, many of whom have difficulties in recognising emotions. The team identified 412 discrete human emotions which they subdivided into one of 24 different groups. Prior to this, psychologists had worked with a standard set of 'Ekman faces' (photographs of the six basic universal emotions developed by Californian psychologist Paul Ekman). The six basic emotions are happiness, sadness, anger, fear, surprise, and disgust.

In a later paper reporting on the outcomes of the 'Mind Reading study, and assessing its effectiveness in teaching adults with Asperger syndrome and high-functioning autism to recognise complex emotions in faces and voices, Baron-Cohen and his colleague Ofer Golan concluded that the integration of emotional information from faces, voices, and context allowed understanding and perception of others' emotions and mental states.[8]

Some 10 years before the study, Baron-Cohen had coined the term 'mindblindness' to describe the inability of some people, particularly those with autism, to 'read' the minds of others.[9] The 'Mind Reading' project was primarily developed for people with autism. However, other applications were considered such as difficult-to-manage children or people with learning disabilities. The term might also be used for anyone who lacks emotional intelligence to the extent that it detrimentally affects their relationships with others.

What does this mean for lawyers?

Emotion recognition is also an important skill for people working in people-centred professions, such as law. It is also highly relevant when dealing with one-to-one relationships and relating within groups. For this reason, social skills training often forms part of management training and is an important part of the national curriculum in mainstream schools in the UK.[10] Despite this, many people experience 'mindblindness', finding themselves unable or unwilling to empathise and to be curious about what they may be thinking or feeling.

A helpful term to cover the capacity to read the mind of another in this way was coined by Elizabeth Meins: 'mind-mindedness'.[11] In a later paper Meins and her colleagues discussed the necessity of a child's own security of attachment for healthy social development and argued that this was enhanced by the caregiver's capacity to treat a child as an 'individual with a mind'.[12] When Beth from our case study began to relate to Steve as an 'individual with a mind', rather than a typical bully, she was better able to read him and the situation generally. Mind-mindedness replaced mindblindness.

Berne's 'parent-adult-child' theory

Before the meeting with Steve, Beth had been reading up on ideas of transactional analysis (TA). As she thought about how she felt about confronting Steve, she came to realise that she had been reacting to him like a cowering child, avoiding conflict and confrontation with an overbearing parent figure. Something about his manner and the way that he dominated the team inhibited her ability to speak up for herself and voice her opinion.

She read about Berne's ideas about the three ego states:

parent, adult, and child (see Figure 1).[13] She realised that, from her point of view, she was reacting in a childish manner. They were both adults and should be relating to each other as adult to adult.

As she prepared for the meeting with Steve, she tried to think of herself as an adult rather than as an apologetic child. With her heart thumping, as she explained herself at the meeting, she felt she vaguely detected Steve's discomfort. What she probably didn't fully realise was that her unexpected assertiveness made Steve feel defensive and infantilised. It was likely *he* felt like the child being told off by a disapproving parent.

In that meeting, something shifted for Beth, not just in terms of a readjustment of respect for her on Steve's part, but something which underscored the way that they related to one another thereafter.

Although her sense of it at the time was imprecise, in the meeting Beth was picking up on Steve's body language, facial

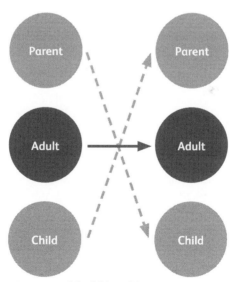

Figure 1: Berne's 'parent-adult-child' model

expressions, and tone of voice. From her assumed position as an adult talking to an adult, she was able to detect something of his emotional reaction, was able to use the greater emotional control in her approach, and a very general sense of Steve's emotion to enable her thinking, understand her own and Steve's emotions, and to manage and control her own emotional reaction. At the outset of the meeting, she had been extremely apprehensive, but at the end she felt a sense of reassurance that she had done the right thing. An exercise based on Berne's TA model is included in Chapter 10, and is designed to help you think about the underlying dynamics of a relationship from the perspectives of both the people involved.

GIVE – Achieving assertiveness

Marsha Linehan, the prime proponent of 'dialectical behaviour therapy', a cognitive therapy, suggests the acronym 'GIVE' to help people think about and manage difficult one-to-one relationships.[14] Assertiveness is achieved by being Gentle, Interested, Validating, and Easy. In the words of an ancient proverb, 'a gentle answer turns aside wrath'. As we see in the next chapter, Beth's assertive discussion with her supervisor led to a subtle change in the working relationships within the team.

References

1. McManus, S., Meltzer, H., Brugha, T. et al, 'Adult psychiatric morbidity in England, 2007: Results of a household survey', The NHS Information Centre, Leeds, 2009.

2. Holmes, J., *The search for the secure base: Attachment theory and psychotherapy*, Routledge, Hove, 2001.

3. Allen, J. G., 'Mentalizing in Practice'. In Allen, J. G., and Fonagy, P. (eds.), *Handbook of Mentalization-Based Treatment*, John Wiley & Sons, Chichester, 2006.

4. Bateman, A., and Fonagy, P., *Mentalization-Based Treatment for Borderline Personality Disorder: A Practical Guide*, Oxford University Press, 2006.

5. Salovey, P., and Mayer, J. D., 'Emotional Intelligence'. *Imagination, Cognition, and Personality, 9*, 1990, pp.185–211.

6. Mayer, J. D., Salovey, P., and Caruso, D. R., 'Emotional Intelligence: Theory, Findings, and Implications', *Psychological Inquiry, 15*, 2004, pp.197–215.

7. Baron-Cohen, S., Hill, J., Golan, O., and Wheelwright, S., 'Mindreading Made Easy', *Cambridge Medicine, 17*, 2002, pp.28–29.

8. Golan, O., and Baron-Cohen, S., 'Systemizing empathy: Teaching adults with Asperger syndrome or high-functioning autism to recognise complex emotions using interactive multimedia', *Development and Psychopathology, 18*, 2006, pp.591–617.

9. Baron-Cohen, S., *Mindblindness: An Essay on Autism and Theory of Mind*, MIT Press, Cambridge, MA, 1995.

10. Baron-Cohen *supra* note 7.

11. Meins, E., *Security of attachment and the social development of cognition*, Psychology Press, Hove, 1997.

12. Meins, E., Fernyhough, C., Russell, J., and Clark-Carter, D., 'Security of attachment as a predictor of symbolic and mentalizing abilities: a longitudinal study', *Social Development, 7*, 1998, pp.1–24.

13. Berne, E., *Games People Play: The Psychology of Human Relationships*, Penguin, London, 1964.

14. Lewis, L., 'Enhancing mentalizing capacity through dialectical behaviour therapy skills training and positive psychology'. In Allen, J. G., and Fonagy, P. (eds.), *Handbook of Mentalization-Based Treatment*, John Wiley & Sons, Chichester, 2006.

Chapter 7:
Team working and
working teams

'One chord is fine. Two chords are pushing it.
Three chords and you're into jazz.'

Lou Reed

Much like a jazz improvisation, groups can be complex, confusing, and chaotic. Thus far, we have thought about ourselves as individuals and in two person relationships. Where three or more people meet to carry out a common task, the potential for creativity and productivity is unimaginable. Alongside this, the potential for complexity and conflict increases exponentially.

Before her confrontation with Steve, Beth's perception of her place in the department was blinkered. Her focus was on getting her work done to the best of her ability, completing her hours (and more), and fulfilling the expectations of the firm. She was vaguely aware that she was being singled out for unfavourable treatment and scapegoated by Steve and, by their silence, the other members of the team. As she was able to think things through more objectively with the LawCare volunteer, she was able to mentalize the one-to-one relationship with Steve, and also to think about her place in the department.

'Interactions in groups are complex to grasp, and identifying specific interventions amidst an almost infinite range of inter-personal and affective communication is such a daunting task as to appear nearly impossible'.[1]

'Successful mentalization (i.e., a "true" understanding of one's own feelings, motives, and thoughts in relation to other minds in specific situations) provides a sense of selfhood, identity, and trust in the capacities of one's own mind. Its opposite, failures of mentalization, might induce confusion, misunderstandings, painful and inexplicable affects, a sense of disorganization and fluctuating self-states, and feeling of detachment from others.'[2]

When groups are working in conditions of extreme pressure, deadlines, with underlying undercurrents of competitiveness and a need to be seen to be performing better than others, rivalries will rumble under the surface. Social dynamics can be particularly confusing when conflict is introduced. It's a bit like trying to follow the track of every moving ball on a snooker table when the cue ball is propelled forcefully into the others. The interaction of the balls is sudden and simultaneous and can only be seen clearly on viewing repeated action replays.

Writing of his experience of captaining the England cricket team and from his later perspective as a psychoanalyst, Mike Brearley says that a captain or analyst's belief that they are fully aware of what is going on can be a self-delusion: 'When such inter-penetrations are happening, it is hard for someone who is caught up in them to see what's going on, much less, without such insight, be in a position to help the patient to understand his behaviour and begin to learn the often powerful reasons for it'.[3]

If one has some internal way of 'pressing the pause button' to control excessive anxiety and overreaction, this creates a space within which one can see slightly more clearly the reality of what may be going on inter-personally and within groups. Without this ability, life can get pretty confusing. (Chapter 9 provides some useful exercises designed to help you 'press pause' and think more clearly.)

Beth's support from the volunteer enabled her to obtain not only personal support, but a forum in which to see what might be going on in her workplace. It certainly helped her to gain a sense of her place in the department and of the unrealistic expectations that she had been placing on herself. Mentalizing has been explained as 'the central mechanism of self-cohesion'.[4] A growing ability to think about her own feelings and motivations and to imagine what might be motivating others in the department enabled Beth to regain a sense of control over herself and her environment.

Talking with the volunteer enabled her to think about herself inquisitively, provide alternative perspectives on what might be going on, challenge her beliefs, share her experience, and reflect on what had been happening in novel ways.

Some basic assumptions

In the late 1940s, working primarily with traumatised ex-servicemen, Wilfred Bion and others at the Tavistock Clinic in London experimented with novel approaches in psychotherapy, particularly in group settings. Bion was a psychoanalyst who had been decorated for bravery in the Great War and one of whose patients was the playwright Samuel Beckett.

While Beckett was articulating his sense of futility and absurdity in the wake of war in plays such as *Waiting for Godot*, Bion and his colleagues grappled with the principles underlying social anxiety. He observed how groups form, interact, and develop as their common purpose emerges. He held that once a group had formed, its primary task was survival.

He contrasted 'working' groups with 'basic assumption' groups. A 'working' group was one in which members predominantly cooperated in working towards the group's aims and objectives. A 'basic assumption' group was one in which the hidden agendas and anxieties of the members interfered with and hindered the group purpose and were diverted to fulfilling the members' own aims and calming their own anxieties. 'Basic' refers to the group's need for survival; 'assumption' relates to the instinctive ways of attempting to assuage group anxieties.[5]

Bion developed his theories over a decade, working with men who had experienced horrific war trauma and observing their interactions within therapy groups. He refined his findings and outlined three 'basic assumptions' that are seen in unhealthy groups; namely, dependency, fight/flight, and pairing:

- We see the assumption of *dependency* playing out where group members consciously or unconsciously allow one individual to make decisions and take the strategic lead.

By default, the group behaves as if it is incompetent and can eventually allow the dominant individual to fail.

- *Fight/flight* can be seen in individuals scapegoating and victimising within the group or withdrawing from the task in hand, becoming passive, avoiding warnings, or dwelling on past history.

- *Pairing* involves individuals joining forces, creating cliques and factions, and redirecting the group's collective goals. There can be an unrealistic optimism that the group will be rescued and in this way its present objectives are avoided.

An organisational analyst looking at the way that Beth's department was and was not functioning, might flag up the way in which the group was operating on a 'fight and flight' assumption. Recognising that group anxieties such as rivalry, humiliation, implied rejection, or maybe the risk of a P45 were feeding into its way of defending itself – by trying to escape from the anxiety by means of inner conflict and displacement of the anxiety by scapegoating Beth (through complicity with Steve's bullying behaviour) – the group was not performing as a 'working' group but as a 'basic assumption' group. While remaining productive overall and 'working' in the sense of completing deadlines and time recording requirements, and keeping clients happy, the group was also operating dysfunctionally at the considerable expense of its members' mental health.

Larry Hirschhorn has proposed additions to Bion's three basic assumptions including the notions of 'covert coalitions' and 'organisational rituals'.[6] By their silence at the way Beth was treated by Steve, other members of the group created a covert coalition which allowed the scapegoating to continue. Essentially, the group used Beth as a dumping ground for their own hidden anxieties. This is the essence of bullying.

Social intelligence

Daniel Goleman who popularised the idea of emotional intelligence, as we saw in the last chapter, has summarised the notion of 'social intelligence' as an overlap of social awareness and social facility. 'Social awareness' refers to a spectrum that runs from instantaneously sensing another's inner state, to understanding their feelings and thoughts, to 'getting' complicated social situations. This includes 'primal empathy' (feeling with others and sensing non-verbal emotional signals), 'attunement' (listening with full receptivity and attuning to a person), 'empathic accuracy' (understanding another person's thoughts, feelings, and intentions), and 'social cognition' (knowing how the social world works).

'Social facility' involves wondering how another person might be feeling, thinking, or intending. Social facility builds on social awareness to allow smooth effective interactions. It includes 'synchrony' (interacting smoothly at a non-verbal level), 'self-presentation' (presenting ourselves effectively), 'influence' (shaping the outcome of social interactions), and 'concern' (caring about others' needs and acting accordingly).[7] Goleman's concept of social intelligence builds on the formulations of emotional intelligence outlined in the last chapter.

As she thought about things after her meeting with Steve, Beth's social awareness and facility grew. She was able to appreciate the pressures that Steve had himself been under and to see things from his point of view. This enabled her to develop a more realistic view of how the department was working and her place within it. It granted her a greater sense of self control, agency, and initiative. Her ability to present herself more assertively enabled her to influence her position in the department, albeit in a relatively modest way. A small step objectively, but a giant leap for her.

As lawyers, we will spend much of our working lives in group settings, in offices, chambers, courtrooms, meetings, mediations, committees, and even in our families. Group dynamics are all around. An ability to 'press the pause button' and step back and wonder what may really be going on around us and under the surface of appearances can help us to understand more clearly. It starts with curiosity.

Groups can be complex, confusing, and chaotic. However, there are ways of simplifying, clarifying, and regaining a sense of control. Sometimes, though, however self- and other-aware we are, however well organised, life throws stuff at us that is overwhelming...

References

1. Karterud, S., and Bateman, A. W., 'Group Therapy Techniques'. In Bateman, A. W., and Fonagy, P., *Handbook of Mentalizing in Mental Health Practice*, American Psychiatric Publishing, Arlington, VA, 2012.
2. *Ibid.*
3. Brearley, M., *The Art of Captaincy: What sport teaches us about leadership*, Pan Books, London 2015.
4. Karterud, *supra* note 1.
5. Bion, W. R., *Experiences in Groups and other papers*, Tavistock, London, 1961.
6. Hirschhorn, L., *The Workplace Within: The Psychodynamics of Organizational Life*, MIT, Cambridge, MA, 1988.
7. Goleman, D., *Social Intelligence: The New Science of Human Relationships*, Hutchinson, London, 2006.

Part 4:
Do

The non-personal *considers our current and past environments, events, and experiences, the things that have happened to and around us, and helps us to make greater sense of them. It also looks at what we can do to alter things in the present and future through changes in attitude, agency, and action.*

Case study 3:
Chris – Environmental stress

This case study is based on the experiences of one or more lawyers, which have been anonymised and rearranged for reasons of confidentiality. It illustrates several common pressures that can impact on lawyers' mental health, which are explored in more detail in the chapters that follow.

The year started well. Unusually, the office party had been a success and his firm seemed to be turning the corner after a difficult couple of years following the recession. Chris was almost on top of his workload and for once did not start January with a sense of foreboding at what the next 12 months might hold. Looking back on the year the following January, Chris described it as his 'year from hell'.

Chris was in his 50s, a partner in a large provincial firm in charge of a department dealing with personal injury and clinical negligence claims. He was reasonably well organised, tried to keep a clear desk, and had a good professional record. Generally, clients' complaints were rare and he made a point of dealing with any dissatisfaction face-to-face with the client.

This had always served him well. He had an open door policy in his department so that staff could, theoretically at least, talk to him at any time about things that were concerning them. If he was not able to deal with things immediately, he would schedule time later in the day or the following day to listen and supervise. Disagreements between team members which happened from time to time were generally dealt with promptly; again, with Chris getting the protagonists together to clear the air with him.

The resignation of a senior fee earner in one of the other departments in January did not create too much pressure for him, but when Joanne, the other partner in his department, announced in February that she was to move to a competitor firm, his heart sank. He knew he would not be able to persuade her to stay and that in a couple of months he would have to break the news to the department.

Chris specialised in clinical negligence work. For the last few months he had been investigating the background of a claim involving a woman in her early 20s who had been knocked down by a car when she was walking home with friends from a night club in the early hours of the morning. She had been admitted to hospital and an overstretched A&E department had not detected a cerebral haemorrhage. The young woman died as a result of the undetected bleed.

When taking instructions from the family, Chris had soaked up a fair amount of the young woman's father's rage at his daughter's death. On one occasion, after the parents had left his office, he felt overwhelmed with sadness. He represented the family at the inquest, which he later described as his 'hardest legal day'. The experience of preparing for and representing the family at the inquest was exhausting.

Shortly after Easter, Chris assembled the department and told them that Joanne would be leaving the following month. This was met with dismay, confusion, and sadness. Joanne had been with the firm for over 10 years and was 'part of the furniture'. Her announcement came out of the blue. For several weeks after this, people popped into his office to talk about Joanne's imminent departure. This was wearing. When she left, he had to supervise her ongoing caseload, involving work that he had been unfamiliar with for some time, including some complex occupational disease claims. He found himself in a difficult position, being asked for advice on technical matters from more junior members of the team, able to give general advice, but not with as much confidence as he would have wished. Work hours increased considerably and he would regularly be at the office for two or three hours longer than everyone else. This continued for several months.

Alongside this, he was coping with family difficulties. In June his elderly mother had a fall and was in hospital for several weeks. He visited her regularly and dealt with her care arrangements on discharge from hospital. Earlier in the year, he had been aware that his daughter who had been engaged for some time was having difficulties in her relationship. In August, his daughter broke off her engagement and returned to live at home for several months.

Later in the same month, when he was on holiday, he learned by text that one of his work partners had died suddenly from a stroke. They sailed together and had been close friends for over 20 years. When he returned to the office after the holiday he was again involved in pastoral work, looking after grieving staff members, while at the same time trying to come to terms with his own deeply felt loss.

Around the time of the funeral, he found that he could not sleep, felt vaguely nauseated throughout the day, and exhausted. He went to see his doctor who suggested antidepressant medication and he started on Prozac. The doctor also suggested referring him for counselling under the NHS, but was told that waiting lists were lengthy. Chris took the initiative and started seeing a counsellor privately; this lasted for around five months. His partners were supportive and in October he was able to take three weeks out of the office to recharge his batteries.

Thinking about this simplistically, in terms of the progression of his experience of stress, Chris moved from the green productive, creative 'prehab' area, through the red excessive stress area until around the time of the funeral when he tipped into the blue zone: clinical depression and burn out. Very little, if anything of what happened during the year could have been foreseen, prepared for, or avoided.

When he looked back on the year he said, 'I could've coped with everything. It was my feelings of helplessness when my daughter's relationship broke up. I think that's what broke me up'.

Chapter 8:
Stuff happens

'How did you go bankrupt?' Bill asked.
'Two ways', Mike said. 'Gradually and
then suddenly.'

Ernest Hemingway, *The Sun Also Rises*

During the course of the year, as events unfolded around and entangled him, Chris's sense of organisation and self-control diminished. Thinking of his sailing experience, he said: 'It was like being out in a storm with a broken mast'. It felt like he was at the mercy of the elements.

The creeping cumulative effect of unwanted changes affected him deeply. Unwelcome events happened to him and around him. From his point of view, it felt like things were being done *to* him. He simply had to react as best he could.

Vicarious trauma

Some years ago, at the start of his career, Chris had stopped doing matrimonial work because he realised that he was losing his objectivity in representing clients. Things came to a head when he realised that he was becoming too involved emotionally in a client's claim for custody of his children. At the time, his daughter was a toddler and he realised vaguely that his natural feelings of parental protection had become entangled with his identification with his client's problems. His intense sense of injustice at his client's position was at odds with the way that he was able to deal with the rest of his caseload. As a result, shortly after conclusion of the case, he stopped doing matrimonial work and began to specialise more in clinical negligence.

During the course of his counselling later in the year, Chris realised that the exhaustion that he felt after the inquest hearing was somehow tied up unconsciously with his feelings for his own, now grown up, daughter and the turmoil that she was experiencing in her relationship. Not only was he carrying the expectations of the deceased girl's family, observing the grief, and sharing their pain, but at another level, he was also experiencing this himself in his anxiety for his daughter. Somehow, the two became inextricably linked.

It is recognised that lawyers who deal with certain practice areas are more at risk of experiencing 'vicarious trauma' or 'compassion fatigue' than others. In certain areas such as family, crime, children, or personal injury work, lawyers have both a professional and pastoral role to fulfil. They are routinely exposed to trauma and, as part of their workload, will listen empathically to their clients' stories and examine heart-breaking and gruesome evidence. It can sometimes be difficult to separate the professional and pastoral roles and one can overspill into another.

Situations can be compounded where lawyers are working under significant time pressures, are overworked, and where caseloads encroach on personal time, leading to feelings of exhaustion and being overwhelmed. Sometimes, disturbing images from clients' stories can intrude into thoughts and dreams and lawyers can begin to see the world as an inherently dangerous place. On one occasion, when Chris was admitted for routine surgery, he realised that he was hyper-vigilant about what could go wrong, at the expense of trusting the surgeon and putting up with routine post-operative pain.

In her 1959 paper 'Social Systems as a Defence Against Anxiety', Isabel Menzies Lyth described how the stresses of nursing and the close relationship it required with patients impacted on the organisation of care, leaving those nearest to patients exposed to emotional pressures that more senior staff and managers were able to avoid.[1]

In common with those on the frontline of the medical profession, nurses were recognised as experiencing high levels of tension, distress, and anxiety. Menzies Lyth wondered how nurses could tolerate so much anxiety. She and her colleagues found much evidence that they could not. Withdrawal from duty was common; one third of nursing trainees did not complete their training, the majority leaving at their own request. It was abundantly clear that significant dysfunctional institutional processes were directly affecting the physical and mental health of junior nurses.

Although removed from physical trauma by several steps, lawyers are also based in situations which are likely to evoke stress. They are in regular contact with clients who are physically ill or injured, often seriously. The outcome of a family dispute or a serious injury claim may be uncertain, and the lawyer has to guide the client through the process. On occasions, as with Menzies Lyth's nurses, 'the work arouses strong and conflicting feelings: pity, compassion and love; guilt and anxiety; hatred and resentment of the patients who arouse these feelings; envy of the care they receive'.

At the time of the inquest, Chris was largely unaware of the unconscious associations between the girl who had died and his feelings for his daughter. These were clarified during the course of the counselling. This enabled him to think about and learn how to contain his own feelings of anger and sadness that he experienced for his daughter. He began to be able to take a more objective view of himself and to see how his experiences earlier in the year had impacted one on the other. In short, he was able to begin to mentalize, to understand something of what had happened to him, and to see the meanings behind this. He learned to identify how his own wishes, feelings, reactions, thoughts, and aspirations for his daughter inter-related at a time when he had so much else on his plate to deal with.

The effects of change

So many things happened during the course of the year, hard on the heels of each other, that Chris really didn't have time to feel that he had dealt with one situation before another presented itself to him. He had experienced a number of losses during the course of the year and had helped others to cope with their losses when he heard of his business partner's death. This took things to a new level.

During the First World War, Freud wrote his seminal paper 'Mourning and Melancholia'.[2] In this he explored the characteristics and process of mourning, grieving after a death or other loss, and the additional aspect of guilt and self-reproach in depressive illness. His view was that the experience of grief – profoundly painful dejection, cessation of interest in the outside world, loss of the capacity to love, and inhibition of all activity – is normal and not pathological.

When Chris's business partner died he felt this to be 'like an amputation'. As if a part of himself was missing. He also felt unaccountably and generally anxious and guilty, although he could not identify why. He later realised that these were aspects of a presentation of clinical depression. There need be no logic behind them.

Writing 30 years after Freud, Kurt Lewin, father of social psychology, speculated about the process of change in a complex paper relating to group dynamics. Lewin proposed that the process of change involved three steps: 'unfreezing, moving and freezing of group standards' (now popularised in the three-phase process of change: unfreezing, changing, and refreezing).[3]

When change occurs in a group setting, the group (1) experiences a form of catharsis which is necessary before prejudices can be reduced, and existing ways of working and values are questioned and *unfrozen*. The group can then (2) *move* and changes can be introduced and new ways of working experimented with. The process of change will then be (3) *frozen* when new ways become embedded and settled within new organisational values which support the new state of affairs.

Although he had little choice in the process, Chris's relatively routine and organised way of dealing with his working life was gradually 'unfrozen' during the course of the year, significant 'movement' and change was forced on him, and his experiences and new ways of working (and in particular thinking about himself and his working environment), were gradually 'refrozen' during the course of and after his counselling.

In the late 1960s, Elisabeth Kubler-Ross, a psychiatrist working with terminally ill patients in Chicago, noticed that in different ways and in varying degrees they grappled with impending death by going through a number of identifiable stages.[4] Kubler-Ross identified the states as denial and isolation, anger, bargaining, depression, and acceptance.

As someone who is approaching death or has suffered a recent loss searches for meaning in the experience, they will experience a chaotic path through the process, or possibly become stuck at one of the stages. As the initial paralysis and shock at hearing bad news subsides, a person may try to avoid the inevitable and unconsciously *deny* the reality of what is happening. Frustrations and *anger* at the situation can then be discharged at anyone nearby. *Bargaining* than follows where the individual tussles with accepting or to denying the reality of what is happening. When acceptance begins to take root, mourning or *depression* can then follow. Sadness is accepted and experienced. Testing and seeking realistic alternatives can then follow and gradually, in a healthy mourning process, an *acceptance* of a new way of living can follow; a way of living with the loss, not denying it.

Loss is part of life. Most of us will experience painful bereavement at some time. Although the death of his business partner shocked him deeply, Chris recognised the most disturbing sense of loss he felt during a chaotic year was for his daughter. He witnessed first-hand her turmoil after the separation and, after the initial shock of the break-up had subsided, he was aware that he felt unreasonably angry at the fiancé whom he perceived had been the main cause of the split.

In therapy, he later realised more clearly that his rage had been bottled up and had, in a sense, been directed inwardly, to his own cost. To his mind, it would of course have been unthinkable for a professional like himself to have squared up to the former boyfriend man to man. Counselling helped him to identify and unpick many of the tightly knotted strands of intra-personal, inter-personal, and circumstantial factors which tipped him into his depressive illness. Although he experienced the therapy as an uncomfortable process, he was able to mourn his way to a greater acceptance of things that he could not change.

References

1. Menzies Lyth, I., 'Social systems as a defence against anxiety', *Human Relations, 13*, 1960, pp.95–121.
2. Freud, S., *Mourning and Melancholia, Standard Edition Volume 14*, Hogarth Press, London, 1917.
3. Lewin, K., 'Frontiers in Group Dynamics: Concept, Method and Reality in Social Science; Social Equilibria and Social Change', *Human Relations, 1*, 1947, pp.5–41.
4. Kubler-Ross, E., *On Death and Dying*, Tavistock, London, 1969.

Chapter 9:
Looking after ourselves

*'They always say time changes things, but
you have to change them for yourself.'*
Andy Warhol

Stuff happens. Things happen around us and to us. Sometimes, we have little or no control over circumstances and events. But there are always things that we can do to improve the situation. Whether you are preparing for a three-hour mock exam or a two-day cross-examination, setting up innumerable completions for Friday or shutting the office door at 10pm, things can be done to prepare for the event.

In this chapter, we will look at six areas in which we can regain a greater sense of agency in professional life. After all, we need to be able to take care of ourselves first before we can think about looking after our clients and others who depend on us.

Five Ways to Wellbeing
The 'Five Ways to Wellbeing' are evidence-based actions which promote people's wellbeing. The activities are simple things individuals can do in their everyday lives. The Five Ways were developed by London-based 'think-and-do tank' the New Economics Foundation from evidence gathered in the UK government's Foresight Project on Mental Capital and Wellbeing. The project, which was published in 2008, drew on research about mental capital and mental wellbeing throughout life. The Five Ways to Wellbeing are a summary of the project's findings.[1]

The Five Ways have been adopted by health organisations, schools, and community projects across the UK and globally to help people take action to improve their wellbeing. They have been used in many different ways; for example, to get people to start thinking about wellbeing, in developing organisational strategy, measuring impact, assessing need, for staff development, and to help people to incorporate more wellbeing-promoting activities into their lives.

The Five Ways are: connect, be active, take notice, learn, and give.

Connect

Evidence indicates that feeling close to, and valued by, other people is a fundamental human need and one that contributes to functioning well in the world. We saw in Chapter 6 that, if we have learned reasonably good ways of 'attaching' to others, we are able to cope with pressures in a more resilient way. It is clear that social relationships are vital for wellbeing and for providing a buffer against mental ill health. Connect with the people around you, with family, friends, colleagues, and neighbours, at home, work or in the local community. Think of these as the cornerstones of your life and invest time in them. Building these connections will support and enrich every day.

Be active

Regular physical activity is linked with lower rates of depression and anxiety. Exercise is vital for slowing cognitive decline as we age and for promoting wellbeing. Discover a physical activity you enjoy and that suits your level of mobility and fitness.

Take notice

Studies have shown that being aware of what is taking place in the present moment directly enhances wellbeing. Appreciating what is happening around us and within us can help us to self-monitor and be more aware of what is really going on in one-to-one and group situations. In essence, the practice of mindfulness is simply about taking notice.

Learn

Continued learning through life enhances self-esteem and encourages social interaction and a more active life. This can be particularly helpful as we approach the end of our professional lives and think about making lifestyle adjustments for life after the office or chambers.

Give

Participation in social and community life has been shown to enhance wellbeing. We saw in Chapter 1 that an altruistic frame of mind can inoculate against mental illness.

Emotional literacy

In Chapter 6, we saw that Simon Baron-Cohen's autism research had identified 412 discrete human emotions which he and his team categorised into 24 groups. These he simplified further to six basic emotions: happiness, sadness, anger, fear, surprise, and disgust.

The aim of Baron-Cohen's research, as noted, was to help those with Asperger Syndrome or high-functioning autism to recognise emotion in people's faces and voices. In the same way, developing a library of words to label the emotions that we experience can enable us to perceive more of what we experience emotionally in day-to-day life. This in turn gives us a greater capacity to be curious about why we might be feeling a particular way, at a particular time. We become more 'emotionally literate'. Emotional awareness can help us to distinguish between the light flurries of anxiety and overwhelming snow-drifts of impending depression.

Coping

How do we cope? Some of us will deal with stresses and strains by setting up an organised working environment. For most, the pressures of legal life will be tolerable and for many, enjoyable. But for some of us the pressures can become impossible.

Like Andrew in the case study, we may find ourselves drinking more to keep anxiety at bay. Or we may self-medicate with non-prescription pharmaceuticals. We may know some of the signs and symptoms of substance abuse, but may be unwilling to accept its increasing influence in our lives. Colleagues may notice that our work is being affected. Family and friends might comment on changes in personal relationships, and we may find ourselves increasingly reluctant to face clients. Hangovers and tiredness may become more regular. We might lie to others about the amount we are consuming, become solitary in our drinking, and feel we have something to hide if people ask us how much we are using. We might become forgetful and miss appointments and deadlines. A reduction in efficiency and ambition might run in parallel with the need to self-medicate to face difficult situations, to calm nerves, and to boost confidence.

Our ways of coping with pressure may not prevent us from tipping into clinically recognisable anxiety or depression. We may choose to ignore signs of anxiety or depression such as changes in sleep patterns, finding it hard to enjoy things, not wanting to see friends and family, eating more or eating less, finding it difficult to make decisions, feeling tired, having thoughts of death, or feeling angry. We may experience tearfulness or have chest pains, low confidence, feel restless, have a racing heartbeat, and sweat more when under pressure.

As we saw in Chapter 4, however, there are effective ways of coping with pressure. Coping styles are automatic psychological processes that protect us against anxiety and from the awareness of perceived internal or external danger. They help to mediate our reactions to emotional conflict. The *Diagnostic and Statistical Manual of Mental Disorders of the American Psychiatric Association* (DSM-IV) divides coping styles into several categories, reflecting mature, immature, and psychotic ways of coping with pressure.[2] We can use the eight mature coping styles as markers for personal wellbeing. These are: anticipation, affiliation, altruism, humour, self-assertion, self-observation, sublimation, and suppression.

Anticipation

We deal with emotional conflict or stress by anticipating the consequences of possible future events and
considering realistic alternative responses. Are we good
at planning our day or the week ahead? Are we able to
anticipate the possibility that our witness will crumble?
How might my colleague respond if I offer constructive
criticism in a particular tone of voice?

Affiliation

We deal with conflict and stress by turning to others for
support. We are able to share problems so that we can
then sort them ourselves, rather than being dependent on
a colleague to dig us out of a hole. Can we trust others
sufficiently to allow ourselves to be vulnerable in this
way? Do we have or can we develop a support network
around us, even one or two colleagues?

Altruism

We deal with stress by looking to meet the needs of
others. The pay-off is when we see others succeed and
quietly share in their happiness.

Humour

We can see direct or amusing aspects of stress. Humour
implies a capacity for realistic and objective appraisal of
ourselves and others and not taking ourselves too seriously. It does not mean being the office joker.

Self-assertion

We deal with things that trouble us by expressing our
feelings or thoughts directly in a manner which is not
manipulative or coercive. With the encouragement and
support she received, Beth was able to behave in this way
with her supervisor.

Self-observation

We are able to cope by reflecting on our own thoughts, feelings, motivation, and behaviour, and responding appropriately. We are able to think about our thinking. This is the essence of mentalizing, outlined in Chapter 5.

Sublimation

We transform negative maladaptive feelings or impulses into socially acceptable behaviour. Maybe, the energy behind the frustration we feel with colleagues or the rage we cannot express against an unreasonable opponent can be channelled into a contact sport or art.

Suppression

We intentionally avoid thinking about difficulties or bad experiences. We learn to count to 10 and rein in impulsive and unhelpful comments or actions.

These qualities are mutually supportive. They are separate ways of coping but they strengthen and complement each another.

Press 'pause'

Like Andrew, you may be sceptical about some of the ideas about mindfulness. You may be suspicious about what is being termed 'McMindfulness', the global commoditisation of an ancient Buddhist practice that seems to offer an escapist panacea to all pressure. Alongside its widespread commercialisation, many have found the practice of mindfulness helpful. As we noted in Chapter 5, the practice of mindfulness has been associated with greater personal happiness, more energy, less anxiety, and a sense of greater control over what happens. Sometimes it's useful to press the 'pause' button and reflect on what's going on.

UK lawyers commonly use time recording units of six minutes. Try out the following focus exercises which can be completed in the same short period of time.

One unit focus

All you have to be able to do is to count up to five. Using the fingers of one hand and spending about one minute on each finger:

1. Concentrate on your *breathing*. Don't try to force anything, just listen to your breathing.

2. Notice any *bodily sensations* that you might be feeling. Go gradually from your toes to the top of your head. Be aware of any feelings of discomfort or pressure.

3. Try to label any *emotions* you may be experiencing. This is likely to be the most difficult part. Emotions are vague and ephemeral. They are likely to merge with bodily sensations, like an anxious knot in the stomach, a tightness of the throat, or pressure in the head. If it's difficult to name the emotions, then maybe think about the six basic emotional labels in the 'Emotional literacy' section above.

4. What are you thinking about? What ideas and *thoughts* are on your mind? Most people will find that during this kind of exercise they will be distracted by thoughts. That's fine. It's normal. When you realise that you have lost concentration, just return to the exercise and allow the thoughts to fall away.

5. Then, for the last minute or so, return to concentrating on *breathing*. Just listen to your breath going in and out.

This exercise can be particularly useful if you are about to go into a difficult or unfamiliar situation, for example an interview, a difficult meeting, or a courtroom. Once you are reasonably familiar with the activity, you can limit the exercise to five breaths, (1) simply being aware of your breathing, (2) a quick body scan for physical sensations, (3) noticing any strong emotion, (4) thinking about your thoughts (although you will probably be thinking so much that you may just be aware of all the thoughts that are around), and (5) return to be aware of your breathing.

One unit 'time' focus

As with the exercise above, this can be done within six minutes. Count the steps off with your fingers if this helps. It can help to regain a sense of perspective on days which are particularly chaotic:

1. Concentrate on your *breathing*.
2. *Past*: Think back about what has happened so far today.
3. *Present*: What's happening now, in this moment? What feelings and thoughts are around? What's happening around me?
4. *Future*: What's planned for the rest of the day?
5. Return to concentrating on your *breathing*. Just listen to the in breath and the out breath.

Just a minute

Focus on your breathing for only a minute. When you become aware of thoughts intruding, just return to focusing on the breathing. It's not as easy as it seems!

Sleep

As we saw in Chapter 1, the recent Bar Council report revealed that over half of barristers do not sleep well. They are certainly not alone. Sometimes, the difficulty is falling asleep after a busy day and working long into the evening. Sometimes, we wake in the middle of the night to find thoughts racing and find we have been unconsciously planning tomorrow's work and worrying about things that didn't get done yesterday. Sometimes, we will wake too early and not be able to get back to sleep. This is a particular problem for perfectionists.

Some simple practical things that we can do might include sleeping in as dark a room as possible. Melatonin, a chemical that regulates the sleep cycle only works when it's dark. Try to get a break from work and have time to relax a bit between working and sleeping. Blue light from iPhone screens, TVs, and computers can suppress melatonin and affect the sleep cycle. Don't drink caffeine too late. (Nag, nag, nag.) There's plenty more information about sleep out there; just Google 'sleep hacks'.

Some say that having a notebook by the bed can be useful. If you wake in the night with your mind buzzing about tomorrow's work and you think you'll forget the indispensable ideas if you go back to sleep, then jot them down on the pad. For some, however, this might make them more awake and they might find it more helpful (and it is my personal recommendation) to remember that the object is to get back to sleep. The intention is to use sleep to recover and forget about the day. One way to tackle this which works for a lot of people is just to concentrate on breathing. Just listen to your breathing. That's all. When thoughts intrude, as they will, simply go back to listening to your breathing. Sometimes, counting on each out breath for up to, say, five breaths can help concentration on the breathing; thinking of a one syllable number is not sufficiently distracting to stimulate other thinking.

Kanban

The idea of kanban was developed in the late 1940s by car manufacturers Toyota. Line workers displayed coloured cards to notify their colleagues down the production line that they needed parts for assembly work. 'Kanban' is a Japanese word for a 'card' or a 'visual signal'. A kanban system is visual and underlies communication within teams so that departments can quickly identify the work that needs to be done and when. It is thought that the human brain can interpret visual information many times faster than text. The system enables a worker to see the big picture and the constituent steps at one and the same time.

Kanban began to be applied to knowledge work in the 2000s, particularly in software development projects. The principles are equally applicable to legal workflows, chambers' administration, and personal organisation. We all have our favourite ways of organising our day-to-day lives. If the way that you organise things is working fine for you, then stick with it. For some though, the legal working day can be a frustrating and chaotic experience. Maybe we are working on drafting an agreement or a statement that requires a full and undivided attention when the phone rings and we can't delay speaking to the caller; then, someone comes into the room for a chat that turns into a 20-minute discussion and we then have to pick up our train of thought 45 minutes later. Sometimes this can be avoided. Sometimes it can't.

One of the benefits of this type of system is to limit the amount of work being processed so that the work that is being done matches capacity. In other words, a lawyer can only handle so much work and simultaneously maintain productivity. When the lawyer or their team or department becomes overloaded with work, everything slows down and bottlenecks develop. A visual system can quickly identify the problem on a kanban board; this could be a physical board on a department wall or simple software for personal or team use. Work can be distributed to other parts of the team or to other days of the week and today's tasks can be focused on. Another aspect of this system is in helping to manage expectations, particularly of clients. It is also helpful for timesheet compliance. Google 'kanban' in images or look up apps and you'll get the picture.

References

1. New Economics Forum, 'Five Ways to Wellbeing'. See: www.neweconomics.org/projects/entry/five-ways-to-well-being.
2. American Psychiatric Association, *Diagnostic and Statistical Manual of Mental Disorders – Text revision* (4th ed.), American Psychiatric Association Press, Washington, 2000.

Chapter 10:
Working well with others

'Remember, teamwork begins by building trust. And the only way to do that is to overcome our need for invulnerability'.

Patrick Lencioni, *The Five Dysfunctions of a Team: A Leadership Fable*

Wellbeing is social; it cannot develop in isolation. Stuff happens to us and around us in the context of our relationships with other people. In this chapter, we will think about practical mentalizing, one-to-one and in group situations.

Reading the changes

If members of his chambers had taken time to notice and think about changes in Andrew's demeanour, and if colleagues in Beth's team, particularly her supervisor, had noticed changes in her productivity and mood, they might have been able to tackle their difficulties earlier, before things got out of hand.

When mental illness develops, changes will be noticeable to a greater or lesser degree by others who work with us. These broadly relate to attendance, productivity, and mood. There may be an increase in unexplained absences or sick leave. People may become more disorganised, work more slowly, and make mistakes more often. There may be a tendency to avoid delegating tasks or to try to work too hard. Stressed staff may become indecisive and decision-making can be impaired. There may be a noticeable increase in dissatisfied clients.

Changes in mood will almost certainly be noticed by co-workers, for example more frequent irritability or tearfulness, overreacting to difficult situations, tiredness or lack of motivation, apparent loss of self-esteem, a tendency to withdraw from social contact, and possibly a lack of interest in self-presentation and appearance. Although normally disguised, there may be increased use of alcohol, drugs, or tobacco.

Breaking the ice

It may be hard to detect these subtle or more obvious changes in co-workers. When noticed, it can be far harder to know how to raise this with the person in question. It can be difficult to know when to time a conversation and far easier to leave someone alone to have an emotion in the corner.

Mike Brearley, writing from the perspective of cricket captain and psychoanalyst, points out that 'a leader or manager in any field, including sport, has to be able and willing to take in and think about the anxiety of those who work in the team. Sometimes, it is a matter of getting to the bottom of an anxiety that has already been covered over. It then has to be conveyed, often subtly, to those in the team that their predicament and anxieties are bearable'.[1]

In other words, a leader or colleague has to be willing to share something of the experience of another and help them think about the anxieties, accept the reality of the stresses, and to think together about how these can be managed. Very rarely can we deal with things in isolation. Andrew was helped by his GP, Beth by her LawCare volunteer, and Chris by his counsellor.

But how do we break the ice? We need to listen. One of the significant contributions of Carl Rogers' 'person-centred' therapy was the introduction of what he termed the three 'core conditions' in the therapist; namely, genuineness, a non-judgemental attitude, and empathy.[2]

That goes for any of us reaching out to help someone we know, maybe a friend or someone we work with. We need to be curious, but not intrusive, about the other person's experience. Even if the response is negative and we are told that they are OK, the ice has been broken and they will know that somebody else is trying to get alongside them and help at a difficult time. We can ask what we might be able to do to help. This will give them space to reflect about what has been going on and what help might be available to them. We can point to help that might be available from other agencies or professionals.

In the likely event that we cannot offer a solution to someone, we can offer support. When Beth talked to the LawCare worker, she was able to gain an alternative perspective on her difficulties. For the first time in ages she was aware that somebody else was taking a genuine interest in what she had been thinking and feeling. This gave a sense of space to be able to reflect on the situation in a more realistic and objective way.

Once the ice has been broken, then practical steps can be considered. Initially, this might simply be a visit to the GP to talk things over or checking out local counsellors.

Dealing with difficult people

George Bernard Shaw observed, 'I learned long ago, never to wrestle with a pig. You get dirty, and besides, the pig likes it'. Dealing with difficult people can be like wrestling with pigs. We can emerge from the encounter feeling emotionally shattered, while they seem none the worse for the experience, or even invigorated by it. But we don't have to wrestle; we can listen and talk instead. We can choose not to go into the sty.

Clients and opponents, and sometimes fellow workers, can demand our time, attention, and compliance. Sometimes, it is appropriate to give it; sometimes, not. When it is inappropriate, there are several ways in which we can choose to respond. We can:

Listen to them
We can give more time to enable them to feel that they have been heard. This on its own can go a long way to diffusing aggression.

Be open
Subject to the standard professional duty of confidence, transparency in the way that we relate to other people can remove

the sense that we have something 'hidden up our sleeve'. Playing cards close to the chest for as long as possible is embedded in litigation culture.

Be assertive
Although she was nervous about the meeting, this worked for Beth. It provides a sense of agency and causes the other person to see that we are taking the initiative and being proactive. It also provides a stronger structure to the relationship. In psychoanalytic terms, it enables one person to feel 'held' or 'contained' (like a child protected by a parent). And sometimes difficult people can come across as toddlers throwing a tantrum.

If it is difficult to be assertive, try the breathing exercises in the last chapter or the two approaches in the next section of this chapter. Your heart may be pounding when you anticipate confrontation, but these approaches may help to ground you.

Be clear
Manage the expectations of the other person. For example, if it is not possible for work to be done within the timescale demanded, make this clear and explain why.

Be reasonable
The issue is the issue. The issue is not me or you.

Stay calm
(As much as possible.) Remember: 'a soft answer turns away wrath'.

Ride the wave
The picture is of a surfer. There may be chaos around but we can learn ways to come out unscathed. Surfing can be scary, but it can also be exhilarating.

Mentalize
Thinking about what the other person may be thinking,

feeling, aiming to achieve in situations where we feel particularly anxious or conflicted will help. Wondering 'Why is this idiot being an idiot with me?' gives a different perspective to the one-to-one conflict. Bullies almost always feel bullied. They are simply displacing the aggression onto someone who they perceive to be lower in the pecking order and more vulnerable. Wonder about what might be tormenting the tormentor.

Adopt other methods of communication

If the person continues to be impossible to deal with, maybe have somebody else speak to them, if this is possible. If the person tries to take a more informal line of communication by phone calls or email, revert to more formalised correspondence and by implication let them know that you are happy for others to see it (for example a supervisor or a judge). Maybe the other person's attempt to criticise you stems from their own fear of criticism.

Press 'pause' again

We have looked at distressed people and difficult people. We will now think about two ways in which we can mentalize in one-to-one relationships. Both are based on some of the theories that we looked at in Chapter 6.

One unit mindreading

Let's say you're talking to a client or colleague and you want to know more clearly what might be on their mind or what they might be feeling. Go through a five-step sequence, using your fingers if you like, to help you to be curious about what might be going on for them:

1. **Breathe**. Firstly, simply be aware of your breathing. This will help focus.

2. **Face**. Secondly, what is the person's face telling you? Particularly the eyes. What emotions might they be experiencing or expressing? How might they be feeling? Be open to different possibilities. We are all opaque.

3. **Voice**. Thirdly, listen. Behind the words, what might be being said? What is not being said? Be sensitive to the tone of voice and wonder what this might say about underlying feelings.

4. **Context**. What else do you know about the person? What is the back story? Think about the context in which the discussion is taking place. What do I know about them already, or what can I reasonably assume? Be curious about body language. Is their posture open or closed? Are actions aggressive or compliant?

5. **Then, just breathe** for a few moments to allow first impressions to settle and clarify.

One unit TA

Here is another five-step sequence to think about the underlying dynamics in the relationship from both persons' perspectives. This is informed by Berne's transactional analysis (TA) parent-adult-child model which we looked at in Chapter 6 and which Beth found helpful:

1. **Breathe**.

2. **Parent**. Is one or other person taking a dominant or dictatorial role in the conversation? Are they being directive? Is this appropriate? Clue: in most adult relationships, adults are expected to act like adults and to treat one another in the same way. This is universal. It includes exchanges between judges and advocates, heads of chambers, clerks and pupils, senior partners and trainees.

3. **Adult**. Are we both behaving as and treating each other as adults?

4. **Child**. Is one person in the relationship taking a submissive role? It is entirely appropriate for people to take orders from those in authority; it is quite another for them to be victimised, humiliated, or bullied.

5. **Breathe**.

If you perceive someone to be behaving in an inappropriately 'parental' or 'childish' way, gently and assertively redress the balance by trying as best you can to behave like a grown up talking to a grown up. This can take time. You may find them infuriating for a while. Practice makes perfect.

Thinking hats

In Chapter 7, we saw that there are ways in which we can recognise if groups are working productively together or if they are dysfunctional. Over the last 30 years, diverse groups from global corporations to children in primary schools have used a method devised by Edward de Bono for using complementary skills and abilities in decision-making. De Bono proposed that decision-making by argument is inefficient, ineffective, and extremely slow. It was never designed to be constructive. This is of course the antithesis of an adversarial approach which comes as first nature to many lawyers. His 'Six Thinking Hats' system is used for group discussion. Alongside a method of parallel thinking, groups can think more effectively and productively in decision-making.[3]

The assumption is that individuals think in a number of distinct ways which can be used to complement one another in looking at strategies and issues from different perspectives. De Bono proposes six discrete ways of thinking to which he attributed 'Hats' of different colours associated with the different approaches:

1. **The White Hat** represents facts and figures, considers information and data, and is neutral and objective. What

do we know? What do we need to find out? How will we get more data?

2. **The Red Hat** symbolises the emotional response. It acknowledges the significance of feelings, intuition, gut instincts, and hunches. What are our feelings right now? What is the gut reaction to this idea?

3. **The Black Hat** symbolises caution and the need to consider difficulties, dangers, and weaknesses in a proposal. It deals with logic and identifying risks and mismatches.

4. **The Yellow Hat** looks at identifying the benefits, positives, and plus points. It represents a hopeful optimistic perspective.

5. **The Green Hat** represents creativity, looking at possibilities, alternatives, and ideas for their own sake without judgement. Statements can be made to investigate an issue or provoke further questions. Discursive random thinking is encouraged.

6. **The Blue Hat** controls the process. It involves thinking about thinking. It facilitates group thinking and discussion and plans for future action. In psychological terms, the blue hat mentalizes the process.

Law firms and chambers that work well will, to a greater or lesser degree, be using the decision-making processes in de Bono's colourful scheme, whether they are aware of it or not. The system is designed to clarify group thinking processes, although individuals' character traits may mean that they typically seem to wear one or two of the hats most of the time. Observing group discussion can be enlightening if we imagine the speaker to be wearing one of the hats. This can also bring into perspective imbalance in a group's approach to the task at hand – and provide a way for this to redressed.

The system also enables parallel thinking, the ability for all group members to look at a particular aspect of an issue from the same point of view, valuing the approach of each coloured hat and what this represents.

Basic assumptions

Using the Six Thinking Hat model is one way of identifying a functional and productive working group. The productive group plays to its mutual strengths, is collaborative and cooperative, and individual perspectives and competences are complementary. Sometimes, groups do not work like this. In Chapter 7 we looked at Bion's group theories. Dysfunctional groups of lawyers may demonstrate characteristics of 'dependency', 'fight/flight', and/or 'pairing'.

De Bono's and Bion's approaches can help us to think about the groups that we work in. A simple way to think about this is to take an A4 sheet of paper. On one side draw three lines to divide the sheet into six rectangles (to represent each of the six hats) and on the other draw two lines to make three rectangles (to represent the basic assumptions). Think about the chambers, partnership, department, or team that you work in. How are we working? Are we competing or collaborating amongst ourselves? Does one member tend to dominate and hold the floor? Are others tending to become factional? Is the meeting guided by a facilitating Blue Hat process or is it led by only one or two Hats? Are group members spoiling for a fight or looking to jump ship? How do we think through opportunities and challenges?

These principles apply in groups of three or more, in families, sports teams, small firms, and mega-firms. They also operate in the overarching legal institutions representing separate branches of the profession, as we will see in the Epilogue.

References
1. Brearley, M., *The Art of Captaincy: What sport teaches us about leadership*, Pan Books, London, 2015.
2. Rogers, C. R., 'The necessary and sufficient conditions of therapeutic personality change', *Journal of Consulting Psychology*, 21, 1957, pp.95–203.
3. De Bono, E., *Six Thinking Hats*, Penguin Books, London, 2000.

Epilogue:
What now?

'Almost all rich veins of original and striking speculation have been opened by systematic half-thinkers.'

John Stuart Mill

When I told one of my lawyer friends that I was thinking of writing a book about mental health and wellbeing in the legal profession, his terse encouragement was, 'Good luck!' I knew his encouragement was shot through with scepticism, if not cynicism, and his view was that I would be wasting my time. Perversely, it was the most useful feedback I received and has informed much of my approach to this book.

Lawyers are far too busy running their practices, ensuring that the briefs keep coming in, earning money, keeping overdrafts under control, supervising staff, looking after clients, keeping up-to-date with law and regulation, and juggling work and family life to be distracted by practical psychology. Maybe the aspiration for a mentally healthy, or even happy, legal profession is an unrealistic, impossible fantasy?

A few years ago, I attended a graduation ceremony at Newcastle University. I was surprised that the chancellor, former Chief Medical Officer Sir Liam Donaldson, gave an address which in the main seemed unduly gloomy for an occasion for celebration. He spoke about the high incidence of depression in young graduates and encouraged students to seek help, rather than suffer in silence. That was in 2009, when the effects of the recession were starting to bite and many students were worried about the challenge of finding a job after university. Unemployment and employment both carry different pressures.

The benefits of good mental health in the workplace impact on practically every area of practice in law firms, including the ability to think clearly and objectively, efficiently, profitably, productively in teams, and effectively in advocacy and negotiations. Recently, the Solicitors Regulation Authority in England and Wales published a revised Competence Statement. Principle five of the statement requires that solicitors provide a proper standard of service for clients. This is approached from four perspectives: ethics, technical skills, self-management, and working with other people. Competence is defined as 'the ability to perform the roles and tasks required by one's job to the expected standard'. Put simply, lawyers are expected to practice law skilfully with personal and social integrity. Integrity involves ethics and health, both mental and physical. Good mental health underpins all four domains of competence.

A recent survey demonstrated that more than two in three legal professionals (73 per cent) are either concerned about or are currently suffering from burnout.[1] The main causes of workplace unhappiness include long hours (58 per cent of respondents), difficult clients (38 per cent), high levels of interruptions each day (35 per cent), low pay (23 per cent), deadline pressure (19 per cent), a lack of autonomy (15 per cent), and the lack of authority (15 per cent). Additional areas of complaint included strained working relationships with superiors, partners, and other colleagues.

The high incidence of mental illness in the legal profession is a 'wicked problem'. It is complex, multifactorial, dynamic, and interconnected. I have attempted to outline a number of the factors, both personal and institutional, which interact and combine to create a professional psychopathology that is so distressing for so many in law.

Heuristics
This book also adopts a heuristic approach. It looks at a

problem – high levels of mental illness in the legal profession – and wonders about causes, contributing factors, legal psychodynamics, and ways of addressing the problem. There is no single simple solution and sometimes the best we can do is to 'muddle through' and to make educated guesses at what might be happening and what can be done about it.

Heuristics are about finding out and discovering, proposing provisional solutions that might be 'good enough'. George Polya, a professor of mathematics at Stanford University in the 1940s, offered a large number of ways in which students could think about problems including working backwards, drawing a figure (diagram) of the problem, and using analogy and example. He also encouraged students to 'look at the unknown'.[2]

The idea of 'reverse therapy' involves working backwards from a known (albeit incomplete) solution (psychotherapy), to better clarify psychological problems to reduce the risk of burnout. We have looked at a number of theoreticians and practitioners throughout this book who have simplified complex human problems into pictures and diagrams. We have also used the experience of lawyers to illustrate the difficulties in day-to-day legal life. Above all, we have tried to look at the unknown, and think about the mystery of the human mind and how we relate to each other.

In 2015, Jonathan Bendor, a professor of political economics and organisations based at Stanford University, published a paper summarising developments in the area of public policy decision-making. His arguments centre on Charles Lindblom's 1959 essay, 'The Science of Muddling Through'.[3] Bendor proposes a heuristic approach to decision-making which is informed by a number of Lindblom's ideas. He proposed a toolkit of heuristics that can be deployed separately and combined in various ways to help with analysis of and to propose solutions for complex wicked problems. The six methods are: decomposition, local search, seriality, multiple minds, imitation, and recombination.

Decomposition
This involves carving off part of a larger problem and sharing out aspects to experts in the relevant fields. We have looked at many aspects of mental health and wellbeing. I have attempted to carve off parts so they can be thought about in isolation.

Local search
Solutions to problems that are radically different to the status quo are bound to be fraught with peril. Bendor recommends searching in the neighbourhood of the status quo. Designs for more effective solutions are easier to adopt than those which are radical and unfamiliar. We have looked at how issues around mental health are being addressed in several jurisdictions, principally in the United Kingdom, the United States, and Australia.

Seriality
Solutions for wicked problems are rarely complete and absolute. The idea of seriality involves small changes being made quickly, iteratively. We don't look to get from A to Z in one go, rather to go from A to G, and then look around and think again and work out how to get from G to R, then think again. As lawyers we can be perfectionists and be uncomfortable with anything less than a complete, ideal solution to our clients' problems or aspects of practice management.

Multiple minds
Having many people working independently on the same problem increases the likelihood of success. I have taken a multidisciplinary approach in looking at the issues. If lawyers wish to enhance wellbeing in the profession, we will have to work more collaboratively. The different branches of the profession have much in common and a great deal of research has been done in recent years by different branches of the profession, in isolation from one another. For professional reasons, this is inevitable and necessary. However, a more co-ordinated approach among the profession should also be effective.

Imitation

This involves looking at what other organisations are already doing in trying to tackle a problem and simply imitating them.

Recombination

Elements from different domains can then be adjusted to create something new. We saw in Chapter 8 Kurt Lewin's simplified breakdown of the process of change. This overlaps with Bendor's methods. Decomposition involves unfreezing, recombination is equivalent to freezing, and the intervening heuristics (local search, seriality, multiple minds, and imitation) are about shuffling and movement.

Lindblom made a particularly valuable observation when thinking about addressing difficult problems: 'That complex problems cannot be completely analysed and that we therefore require strategies for skilful incompleteness still seems close to obvious to me'.[4] He also modestly pointed out that he only had a weak grasp of the concepts that he discussed. We also may have a weak grasp of some of the concepts discussed in this book, but this need not inhibit us from 'muddling through'.

Managing change

The process of unfreezing, moving, and freezing is disruptive. We met Isabel Menzies Lyth when we were thinking about nurses' experience of vicarious trauma.[5] Writing after several decades working as a consultant advising on organisational change in the health service, in an essay entitled 'A psychoanalytical perspective on social institutions', she made a number of pertinent observations about managing the process of change in institutions.[6] To my mind, her observations on the medical profession are equally applicable to law, and some of these are explored under the headings below.

Coping styles

Whether it is wholesale or iterative, change in a social institution 'inevitably involves re-structuring the social defence system and this implies freeing underlying anxieties until new defences or, better, adaptations and sublimations are developed'. We have seen that as individuals we instinctively defend ourselves against anxiety by adopting our own coping styles. Altering attitudes and practices about wellbeing can involve anxieties about weakness, stigma, shame, and avoidance. Lawyers can be more vulnerable than others in certain areas. We saw that the law can attract people with certain personality traits – perfectionist, generally risk averse, cautious – who find it difficult to be seen as failing. And perceived social status and a 'need to be needed' by our clients may prevent many of us from acknowledging some deep anxieties.

Catastrophe

'There is a sense in which all change is felt as catastrophic even when it is rationally recognised as for the better, since it threatens the established and familiar order and requires new attitudes and behaviour, changes in relationships, and a move into a comparatively unknown future.' We saw that the experience of loss is a particularly uncomfortable and fluctuating process. As lawyers, we can be more comfortable with a traditional, self-contained, and reserved way of working.

Contact

'Some of the changes that institutions make actually bring their members into more direct and overt contact with difficult tasks and stressful situations than before.' The process of learning to be assertive with an overbearing supervisor can be uncomfortable. Thinking about unseen mental illness carries an implication that it could happen to anyone, including me.

Confrontation

'This is a potentially maturational experience for the members who "learn" to confront reality and deal with it more effectively.' Individuals become more resilient; institutions also. Much is being done at present to make workforces more resilient, and law firms are also beginning to catch on: awareness training for staff and managers, links with local counselling and psychotherapy providers, development and implementation of mental health and wellbeing policies, employment assistance programmes and mentoring, self-help resources, the practice of mindfulness, flexible working practices and more open cultures within workplaces, a reduction in unnecessary out of hours emails and the expectation that they will always be answered promptly, mental health first aiders, the creation of mental health champions, and (probably at the top of the list) enthusiastic buy-in from senior management. Tackling the challenges to wellbeing will lead to a more mature profession.

Containment
'While change is taking place the problem of containment is central: the presence of someone who can give strength and support, help manage the anxiety, continue the process of developing insight and help define the exact nature of the desirable changes.' Menzies Lyth was concerned that business consultants should not simply confine themselves to analysis of individuals' roles in the business and corporate structure, but that they should be thoroughly observant of the psychological processes working within an organisation. 'Consultants who lack a psychoanalytic orientation may well confine themselves to role and structure without sufficient understanding of the contribution to them of unconscious content and dynamics. They may suggest changes in role and structure without the backing of the requisite changes in work culture.'

Culture shifts
'Work culture analysis… considers such things as attitudes and beliefs, patterns of relationships, traditions, [and] the psycho-social context in which the work is done.' A recent survey carried out by UK firm gunnercooke revealed that ingrained aspects of work culture were factors leading to lawyer

burnout. The aspects include lawyers' obligation to record time and make every single minute count, inflexible working patterns, lack of control over workload, poor work-life balance, and long working hours.[7]

This experience is reflected in the financial sector, where similar expectations are institutionalised. There is a clear tension between the demands of this culture and life outside work. For some, it pays off; for others, they drop off. Fuel to the fire or burnout. 'A banker's wife... had worked in the financial sector and understood the pressures and the pay-backs [for her husband]'. She said, 'I know what it's like for him. I used to work at a "magic circle" law firm myself. I have pulled all-nighters, worked till one at night for weeks on end. I remember exactly how it works, how you become one with the team, this feeling of: we're going to do this, and we are going to win because we are the best.'[8] Clearly, in a global practice, being in the middle of Far East and US time zones stretches the day at both ends.

Some lawyers have broken the mould and have created a new culture. Clearly, those in smaller firms or chambers have more flexibility to pivot and change direction, sometimes diametrically. Australian lawyer Michael Bradley left a large Sydney firm to help set up his own practice, Marque Lawyers. His opinion is simple; namely, that nothing will change until the business model changes. He is polemically critical of legacy firms whose model is based on strict adherence to the timesheet and where 'the mindless pursuit of profit is an end in itself'.[9] The firm is growing and Bradley is clear in his direction: 'the truth is that having fun has been one of [our] values since we started, and we remain violently committed to it'. Bradley has expanded on his ideas of doing law in new ways in a recent book in which he notes that, in Australia, private practice lawyers suffer depression and anxiety at about four times the rate of the general population.[10]

Collaboration
'Work culture analysis... considers ...the psycho-social context

in which the work is done and how people collaborate in doing it'. We noted above that there is the possibility of significant advance in addressing wellbeing issues in the legal profession if there is greater cooperation and collaboration between professional bodies. We may be different branches of the tree but we share the same trunk and roots. We are dependent on and nourished by the same source.

What is to be done?

The recent report commissioned by the Bar Council in the UK concluded with a number of practical proposals for enhancing wellbeing at the Bar.[11] In my view, the ideas are equally applicable to other branches of the profession, and I have been mindful of them in writing this book. The suggestions include those outlined below.

Cognitive style

The report recognises that lawyers have a perfectionist streak and sometimes have unhelpful patterns of thinking. (We looked at this in Chapter 2.) It suggests that cognitive tools and learning could be provided to those working in the law to deepen and further build levels of resilience. In Parts 2–4 of this book, I have suggested a simple yet comprehensive way of thinking about the individual, social, and circumstantial aspects of legal life: 'Me.You.Do.'

Stigma

It is hoped that work carried out through a wellbeing programme will lead to reduced stigma around workplace stress.

Mentoring

Mentoring appears to have a significant positive impact and so a formal programme to build this source of support is a clear opportunity. Lessons can be learned from good practice in mentoring where this is already taking place. We have seen the examples of Andrew, Beth, and Chris, who were all helped by mentors in different contexts. It is only regrettable that they received this support at the rehab rather than the prehab stage.

Social support

Leadership capability could be enhanced to capitalise on the social support reported and valued within the profession 'alongside knowledge and skills in relation to other constructs for intrinsic motivation, engagement and cognitive capacity and efficiency'.

Remuneration, work-life balance, and workload

A review of the remuneration structure at the Bar is suggested, as is further analysis in relation to work-life integration and workload capacity. I regret I can offer no words of wisdom on better remuneration. The lawyer case studies say something of difficulties with work-life balance and how this can be better achieved. The issues surrounding workload capacity are outlined above.

Psychological health support

LawCare's role in providing help to the legal profession at times of need has been illustrated at some length. Please refer to the 'Advice and support' section below for further details about LawCare and other organisations who may be able to help.

The missing metric

In his 2013 report for the Centre for Economic Performance,[12] Professor Richard Layard noted that, since the Second World War, most advanced countries have made huge strides in addressing a broad range of social ills, such as poverty, poor education, and disease. He noted, however, that past social reformers and research into misery and happiness had overlooked 'the human factor – the problems that come from inside ourselves'. In short, mental health. This, he said, is a major factor in production, and the biggest single influence on life satisfaction.

He concluded his report by making a number of policy recommendations, and in particular underlined the need for parity of treatment for mental and physical illness. He concluded by saying that, if we want to improve the wellbeing of our society, we need a change of tack. 'Economic growth is not the magic bullet and happiness depends more on the quality of relationships and our own inner peace. Mental health is vital for both of these. Improving it could be the most important single step forwards in the 21st century.' This is equally true for lawyers.

Healthy justice depends on healthy lawyers.

References

1. Manglani, M., 'Two in three UK lawyers are facing burnout', *Managing Partner, 18*, 2015.
2. Polya, G., *How To Solve It: A New Aspect of Mathematical Method*, Princeton University Press, 1945.
3. Bendor, J., 'Incrementalism: Dead yet Flourishing', *Public Administration Review, 75*, 2015, pp.194–205.
4. Lindblom, C. E., 'Still Muddling, Not Yet Through', *Public Administration Review, 39*, 1979, pp.517–526.
5. Menzies Lyth, I., 'Social systems as a defence against anxiety', *Human Relations, 13*, 1960, pp.95–121.
6. Menzies Lyth, I., 'A psychoanalytical perspective on social institutions', In *The Dynamics of the Social. Selected Essays, Vol. 2.*, Free Association Books, London, 1989.
7. Manglani, M., 'Two in three UK lawyers are facing burnout', *Managing Partner, 18*, 2015.
8. Chapman, L., 'Stress in the City', *Therapy Today, 23*, 2015.
9. Bradley, M., 'Marque Lawyers – The development of law firm innovation', Case study 2 in *Law Firm Innovation: Insights and Practice*, ARK Group, London, 2015.
10. Bradley, M., *Kill All the Lawyers: The Decline and Fall of the Legal Profession*, Hampress, 2012.
11. Positive, *Wellbeing at the Bar: A Resilience Framework Assessment (RFA)*, 2015.
12. Layard, R., CEP Discussion Paper No 1213, 'Mental Health: The New Frontier for Labour Economics', Centre for Economic Performance, London, 2013.

Recommended further reading

ME – Resources to promote self-awareness

Grosz, S., *The Examined Life*, Random House, London, 2013.
Tales of psychotherapy in short-story format, based on the author's 25 years as a practising psychoanalyst.

Perry, P., and Graat, J., *Couch Fiction: A Graphic Tale of Psychotherapy*, Macmillan, Basingstoke, 2010.
Therapy in graphic novel format, starring a barrister client.

Allen, J., Bleiberg, E., and Haslam-Hopwood, T., *Understanding Mentalizing: Mentalizing as a Compass for Treatment*, Bull Menninger Clin 67, 2003. pp. 1–11. Available at: www.menningerclinic.com/education/clinical-resources/mentalizing.
A short and lucid overview of the theory and practice of mentalization (a handout for participants in the Professionals in Crisis programme at the Menninger Clinic, Houston).

Freeman, D. and J., *Anxiety: A Very Short Introduction*, Oxford University Press, 2012.
Pithy overview of recent theory and practice, including how Michael Palin deals with stage fright.

Williams, M., and Penman, D., *Mindfulness: A Practical Guide to Finding Peace in a Frantic World*, Piatkus, 2011.
Introduction to mindfulness with a CD of guided meditations.

YOU – Resources to promote inter-personal awareness

Skynner, R., and Cleese, J., *Families and How to Survive Them*, Methuen, London, 1983.
Co-authored by another Python – accessible and entertaining primer from the 1980s on how we relate.

Pease, A. and B., *The Definitive Book of Body Language*, Orion, London, 2004.
Pictorial introduction to listening by looking.

Berne, E., *Games People Play*, Penguin, London, 1964.
The roles we adopt and the games we play in day-to-day life.

De Bono, E., *Six Thinking Hats*, Penguin Books, London, 2000.
Argument is 'inefficient, ineffective and slow', argues de Bono. Adversarial lawyers might argue with this. A way to understand where others may be coming from and to facilitate group perspectives.

DO – Resources for individuals and organisations with actionable guidance on managing stress and promoting positive mental health

Cooper, C., and Kahn, H., *50 Things You Can Do Today to Manage Stress at Work*, Summersdale, Chichester, 2013.
Practical bullet points for coping with work and life.

Mental Health First Aid, 'The Line Managers' Resource', 2013.
Available as a free download at: mhfaengland.org/workplace/line-managers-resource.
Practical guide to managing and supporting people with mental health problems in the workplace.

ACAS, 'Promoting positive mental health at work', 2014.
Available as a free download at: acas.org.uk/mentalhealth.
Guide for employers and line managers, intended to help them to understand mental health and its impact on individuals and the organisation.

Glossary

Affect (affective)
Emotion (relating to emotion).

Alexithymia
Difficulty in reading one's own and others' emotions. Literally: 'a-lexi-thymia'; without words for emotion.

Coping mechanisms
AKA 'defence mechanisms'. Instinctive ways in which we cope with anxiety. Some work better than others. They help us to experience what we sense to be the lesser of the evils.

Heuristic
Getting to 'good enough' provisional explanations on the basis of limited or contradictory data.
Forming informal working hypotheses.
Guessing at solutions to problems by rules of thumb.
Muddling through.

Intra-personal
What goes on in my mind.

Inter-personal
What goes on when minds meet, one-to-one and in groups.

Mentalization
Minding minds.

The ability to reflect realistically on intra- and inter-personal interactions.

The ability to see oneself from the outside, and others from the inside.

Thinking about feelings, and feeling about thinkings.

Attending to states of mind in self and others.

Holding mind in mind.

Seeing me; seeing you.

Me.You.Do
A simplified way of understanding intra-, inter-, and non-personal interactions and demands.

Being mindfully aware of what is happening *within* me, *between* me and others, and *around* me.

Mindblindedness
An inability to adequately empathise and think about others' thinking.

Mind-mindedness
The reverse of mindblindedness.

Mindfulness
Self-awareness at this moment.

Paying attention to and noticing what is happening now.

Prehab
Mindful preparation for stuff that happens.

Psychodynamics
(Literally: mind-forces). The interplay of psychological forces that underlie human behaviour, relating, thinking, and feeling and their relationship to early, current, and anticipated experience.

Psychotherapy
Rehabilitating by talking.

Most forms of psychotherapy have common, contrasting, and complementary aspects.

Reflective function
The ability to think realistically about states of mind in self and others.

Rehab
In a therapeutic setting, mindfully sorting the mess of stuff that has happened.

Resilience
An ability to bounce back.

Reverse therapy
Applying the principles of psychotherapy before rehab.

Wicked problems
Complex social problems which appear insoluble. They can only be tackled by chopping them into manageable bits.

Advice and support

Urgent help

LawCare

Free helpline: 0800 279 6888

(9.00am to 7.30pm weekdays and 10.00am to 4.00pm weekends and public holidays)

lawcare.org.uk

LawCare was established in 1997 to provide support to members of the legal professions in the UK and Ireland facing personal and professional problems. The helpline is free and completely confidential.

It is a registered charity and works throughout the UK, Isle of Man, and the Republic of Ireland. Support is available to students, those in training, legal professionals, support staff, and their families. The helpline operates 365 days a year. Trained staff and volunteers who take the calls have worked in the law and understand the demands of a legal career.

Samaritans

samaritans.org

08457 909090 (UK); 116 123 (ROI)

24-hour help and advice for out of hours when LawCare's phones are off the hook.

Counsellors

If you think you might be helped by talking things through with someone, check out the sites below. I would recommend you seek a therapist who is accredited by one of the professional bodies. This is a mark of experience and commitment to recognised standards.

UK/Britain: British Association for Counselling and Psychotherapy
bacp.co.uk/seeking_therapist/right_therapist.php
United Kingdom Council for Psychotherapy
members.psychotherapy.org.uk/findATherapist

Ireland/Northern Ireland: Irish Council for Psychotherapy
psychotherapy-ireland.com/find
Irish Association for Counselling and Psychotherapy
iacp.ie/about-irish-association-for-psychotherapists-counsellors

Online resources
LawCare's website
lawcare.org.uk
Jam-packed with helpful information for lawyers' wellbeing
and practical guidance.

The author's site
guslyon.com
Pointers to resources and ongoing informal exploration of
wicked problems, prehab, and Me.You.Do.

The Bar Council's wellbeing page
barcouncil.org.uk/supporting-the-bar/wellbeing-at-the-bar
Counsel for counsel.

Mind
mind.org.uk
Lots of information about wellbeing from the mental health
charity, Mind.

The Royal College of Psychiatrists
rcpsych.ac.uk/mentalhealthinformation.aspx
Resources and information from The Royal College of
Psychiatrists. Also check out the 'Work and mental health' tab
on the same page for guidance on workplace issues.

Healthy workplaces

There is a vast amount of information online covering personal wellbeing and healthy workplaces. If you want to explore further, you might like to try:

NHS: nhs.uk/Livewell/mentalhealth/Pages/Mentalhealthhome.aspx
Health & Safety Executive: hse.gov.uk/stress
ACAS: acas.org.uk/index.aspx?articleid=1361